# Postcards

# from the

# Widows' Path

# Postcards from the Widows' Path

## Gleaning Hope and Purpose from the Book of Ruth

Ferree Hardy

Cover design and layout by Greyden Press.

ISBN: 978-1-57074-032-9

Printed in the United States of America

*To*
*Bruce and Tom*

If your law had not been my delight, I would have perished in my affliction.          Psalm 119:92

# Contents

# Foreword

In the pitch blackness of grief and widowhood, this book is a beacon of light that illuminates the path of hope. Ferree's wisdom, honesty, humor, and conversational tone makes us feel like we're having coffee with a dear old friend, crying and laughing and trying to make sense out of our devastating loss. And she does just that. She makes sense out of it. By exploring the Book of Ruth, Ferree shows us the biblical model of how three women responded to the pain of losing their husbands. Come inside for a while... get yourself a cup of coffee and a comfy seat, and let Naomi, Ruth, Orpah, and Ferree show you God's love, God's plan, and the special place God has in his heart for widows. This is a journey you never would've chosen, but it's a journey you'll never regret... if only you trust God to bring many blessings from your brokenness. How I wish I'd had this wonderfully encouraging, valuable book in the weeks and months after my own husband's death on 9/11. Nevertheless, I'm thrilled to have it now, and it is a treasure I can share with every new widow I meet.

Jennifer Sands
9/11 Widow
Christian Author and Speaker

# How to Use This Book

A widow who's been there, who was shocked by the struggle and certain of despair, penned this book you are reading. Even when she was sure she couldn't take it anymore, she held on anyway and kept knocking away on God's door. Although God never answered with the cozy peace and comfort promised by loads of sympathy cards, one day when she tried the doorknob to God's house, it turned. That door creaked open to the ancient book of Ruth. The widow entered and found herself drawn into a world of timeless truth, a story of real widows just as fresh and practical as any living today.

I was that widow.

I discovered that the book of Ruth captured the ever-changing landscape of grief, the various ways people process grief, the plethora of choices for widows, and the amazing love and relationship God has in store for all of us. The book of Ruth answered my questions through a story, without ever wagging a "you ought to... you should..." finger at me.

There are many ways to read *Postcards from the Widows' Path*, and I hope you'll return to it many times—that it will serve as your own walking companion through the valley of the shadow of death.

Please don't think you must read it cover to cover.

Instead, in the early days of widowhood, I advise you to only read the "postcards" at the beginning of each chapter. These imaginary little notes from the widows in Ruth will settle in your soul and give you hope for the day.

If you're interested in my personal story, you'll find it comes next in "How This Book Came About." If you're family, I'm sure it'll make you cry, so don't say I didn't warn you! You might not agree with my recollections because they don't match your own or how you thought I was doing, but this is the story of my private and inner struggle and how God's Word sufficiently seeded hope, and has since brought it forth abundantly. The last person I intended to write about, however, was me! So I don't mind at all if anyone skips my introduction. The important part is the story of Naomi and Ruth.

After the postcards, when you're ready to give it a try, read chapter by chapter, at your own pace. Thoughtfully consider the journaling exercises at the end of each chapter. Writing things out is a big help in grief. You can write directly in the book, in a journal, or—in my personal favorite, an inexpensive 4"x6" spiral notebook that you can find at any discount store. If you choose this option, you'll find it's just the right size to tuck in your purse or carry alongside your Bible.

The journaling exercises will provide you with a marvelous record of your transformation. (I like that word so much better than "healing," for grief is not a disease!) Months from now, when you reread what you wrote, you'll be filled with wonder at the work God has done in your life and in you.

There is a five-part discussion guide for *Postcards from the Widows' Path* at my blog, www.widowschristianplace.com. Why not gather a few other widows together once a week or once a month and select a couple of the questions to chat about? Provide a pot of coffee or some hot tea in the winter, a chilled beverage in the summer, accompanied by a box of tissues and a willingness to share, and you'll be giving yourself and others a true and much-deserved gift—the treasure of deep, lasting friendships.

Speaking of friendship, I encourage you to visit my blog. You'll find helpful articles, links to grief support groups and widows ministries, and me! I'd love to hear from you, and we can all learn from and lean on each other!

❤ Ferree

# How This Book Came About

"Do you want to see him?" the emergency room doctor asked after he stepped into the Quiet Room of the hospital and awkwardly said, "I'm sorry. There was nothing we could do."

I was sitting there with my son Brad, an eighth grader at the time, and two or three leaders from my church. We were in that suspended moment of disbelief that exists somewhere between hearing the reality and grasping it. No one could speak for what seemed like an eternity. Then, I finally said it myself. Incredulously, I managed to blurt out the D-word:

"Do you mean he's...*dead?*"

"Yes, I'm sorry. Do you want to see him? I'll get a nurse." The doctor said, hurrying out before I was aware that I'd even answered him.

I could only assume I must have nodded or somehow croaked a feeble, "yes."

I felt numb and smothered. Hardly an hour ago, Bruce had come home from the church office, hugged me in the kitchen while I was making supper, and gone downstairs to do some weightlifting. Brad and I heard a yell, and then our house grew too quiet. I found Bruce lying on the floor. I thought he was playing a practical joke on me and waited for him to start laughing, but he didn't move. I yelled to Brad and my daughter, Lisa, to call 911, I heard the sirens, got out of the way of the EMT's, watched them carrying the love of my life out on the stretcher, and...now this.

Suddenly, a nurse appeared, and I was interrupted from my shock by a wave of murky colors: her brown, curly, shoulder-length hair and her sickening, sea-green scrubs. *Why do they allow that color in a hospital?* I wondered. I squinted to see her eyes, nose and mouth. I wanted to see if she was a real person, someone I could hang on to, but my vision blurred, and she remained faceless.

I was standing, but I felt like I was under water with ears plugged and eyes blurred. The nurse's words came out of her mouth in heavy cartoon bubbles, slow as taffy oozing out of an extruder. I have no idea what she said. The only sound was my heart beating in my ears: *thump-thump...thump-thump...* I kept forgetting to breathe. Nurse Sea Green motioned for me to follow her, then turned to lead the way down a wide hospital corridor. Moving with slow, liquid motions, we entered an area filled with empty hospital gurneys strewn helter skelter, like emptied grocery carts abandoned haphazardly in a parking lot.

We zigzagged around the labyrinth of vacant gurneys and faced a dismal curtain.

"Read-y?" the nurse asked in her distorted voice. Before I could tell her that I wasn't ready at all, I'd never be ready, she twirled back the curtain and stood aside to watch me.

Several beds were side by side, their starchy-stiff white sheets pulled tight on all except one: the one with a body. There he lay, as if he was in storage, with one of those stupid, super-sized paper towels covering everything but his face: my husband, my pastor, my very best friend, my love. . . my Bruce.

His eyes were closed, and he was absolutely, eerily still. I leaned in and waited for his eyelashes to flutter like they always did when I neared him in his sleep. He had always been able to sense my presence, even in the deepest of his dreams, but not this time. Placing my hand on his chest was like holding a seashell; he was empty and hollow inside. I kissed his cheek, and it was cool and lifeless to my lips.

"He's gone," I whispered. I don't know how long I stood there, but it was long enough for half of me to lie down on the gurney and curl up next to him. The other half of me walked out of the hospital into a night of cold, February rain.

I don't know why the house was standing when Brad and I got home. I don't remember who drove us home, nor do I remember walking inside. I almost remember telling my daughter Lisa, who had stayed home to man the phone, seeing her questioning face as she hurried to meet us when we came in the door. But my mind stops there, blocking the heartbreak of her realization—something I don't think any mother would ever want to remember. I remember phoning my oldest daughter, Brooke, a sophomore at Moody Bible Institute in Chicago, where Bruce and I had met. I don't recall what I said to her, but I'll never forget the wail I heard on the other end of the line. The memory knocks me to my knees even today.

The next morning, incidentally my forty-fourth birthday, dawned as my first full day of widowhood.

Days later, we found out Bruce's cause of death. A brain aneurysm had taken my husband, and just like that, life as we knew it, along with all our dreams, came crashing down for my children and me.

Scenes like this reel out for thousands of other wives, mothers, and children around the world every day. Are you one of us? Do you wonder where to turn? Where do you even start? How can you live without the one person you can't live without?

Here, my friend. Hold onto my hand, and we'll go through this together. Can I tell you a secret? I didn't think I'd make it either.

Questions and uncertainties bombarded me after the funeral. Mind-numbing shock and body-shaking crying spells stifled me with their demanding intensity. If I had the rare pleasure of sleep, when I opened my eyes in the morning, the instant reality of the empty side of the bed groaned. Well-meaning people unintentionally added to the pounding, always asking the worst question, the loaded, "How are you?" I wondered, *Why does everyone ask me that, relentlessly, one after another? Do they actually want me to answer that with more than, "I'm fine, how are you?"*

Could I really tell them their seemingly innocent "How are you?" hung me on a pendulum that swung back and forth, from choking back tears of razor-sharp pain to moments of hysterical appreciation for the littlest things: a shaft of sunlight breaking through a cloudy day, the purple crocuses poking open a circle around the birdbath outside my kitchen window, or the sound of a slamming car door that announced Brad and Lisa were home from school? Did they really expect or want to open me up like that? Or were they asking for the sake of their own reassurance, questioning whether or not they'd survive the day when their turn at widowhood came?

I don't remember what I mumbled to placate people, but everyone marveled at the peace they thought they saw.

If only they'd truly understood grief. It was physically and mentally impossible for me to explain to each person how I really, truly felt, for I didn't even know myself. I didn't know if I'd make it, and I certainly couldn't reassure them that they would.

I only knew two things: One, I was on the wildest roller coaster ride of my life; and two, I was expected to function—to wake, dress, eat, work, and sleep—as if nothing in my life had changed, as if things were normal and life hadn't become surreal. Imagine getting dressed on a roller coaster! I could hardly decide which foot went into which shoe, and to top it off, I had to put that shoe on while hanging on to one crazy, jolting ride. The assumed strength and peace were not that at all; they were simply shock and numbness. I was emotionally paralyzed and could hardly think.

I was no longer the pastor's wife, my high calling and privilege. That was a loss too—a huge personal loss! Still, I loved my church as always, perhaps even more so. I needed to be there, too, even though the void in the pulpit and the absence of Bruce's bright smile ripped my heart out as I sat there amidst the congregation that he'd once shepherded. The church took good care of me and patiently allowed me to grieve. As much as I appreciated them, however, my husband was gone. After a few months, I needed someone to talk to. I couldn't tell my church people *everything*.

As much as possible, I had lived my life as an open book, transparent and available. Nevertheless, I suppose most pastors' wives develop coping skills and rationales for living in a virtual fishbowl. For me, I took on the role of a mother. As a mother, I didn't share all my pain and questions with my children. Sometimes I want to shield them from the struggle, and at other times, I don't know how to explain or describe what I'm going through. Likewise, I shared what I could with my church, but I didn't tell them everything. What I couldn't tell to anyone else on earth, I tried to discuss with God.

Unfortunately, God didn't seem to listen. Months passed, and my tension only worsened. My expectations of God and his actual response differed so greatly that I saw two completely different pictures in my mind.

I first pictured a big, cozy quilt of comfort snuggled around my shoulders, held in place by God's warm hand. *Why should I be sad? Why should grieving take more than a few weeks? My husband is in heaven, and we'll be reunited someday.* Greeting card theology billowed out promises of peace, loving memories, and caring friends. *That's what I'm entitled to, right? Christians are supposed to get heaping helpings of peace and comfort... aren't they?*

But that wasn't what I got.

Instead, another image appeared. I saw myself as a four-year-old little girl swinging in a Kool-Aid kid backyard with her best friend on a happy summer day. But then I heard a door creak open, and God's big feet, dressed in the most hulking leather work boots I could ever imagine, stomped out of his stately house next door and came into my yard. With one huge hand, he lovingly scooped Bruce up to be with him, and with the other, he clenched a fist and punched me off the swing.

I flew through the air and crashed on sharp stones, leaving my knees and hands scraped and bloodied, inlaid with dirt and small stones, and my lip cut and gritty. I heard myself sobbing—a brokenhearted little girl who had never known such pain before, stunned that her loving Father God would do such a seemingly cruel thing to her. Then I heard the sound of footsteps walking away from me. The door to God's nice house slammed shut, and the deadbolt clicked, locking me out. I felt abandoned.

To look at me, though, everything seemed fine. Friends fluttered around like butterflies, checking on me. They saw that I exercised a lot. I traveled more than usual with the kids and spent extra time with faraway family. I busied myself with housework, paying the bills, and developing friendships with some amazing people God sent my way.

But inside, the tension between the cozy quilt of comfort and getting punched out by God grew stronger. An undercurrent of panic began to flood me, and my whole body tensed and strained, torn between fight and flight. The unanswered questions continued their demanding line-up every morning.

As the months passed, I still felt like half a person. God's silence— and Bruce's—were all I heard.

\* \* \*

I never wrestled with *Why? Why did my husband die?* God spared me that torment. Besides, deep down, I suppose I knew that from my perspective, there was no explanation that would satisfy me or make it worth the suffering of my children. *Kids need two parents. The world needed Bruce's talents—his wonderful way with words and people, his Bible-teaching, his humor, his music, his friendship, and his love.* I sensed that asking why Bruce had died would have been nearly irrelevant. It was a question that just didn't fit earth's plane of reality. Instead of *Why did Bruce die?* I wrestled with, *Why am I left here? What will I do now? How can half a person exist?*

Looking for answers, after the first year of Bruce's death I attended a grief workshop that met weekly at a nearby church. It helped in many ways—not enough, but many. I knew dark and slippery feelings lurked in my heart, too elusive to capture and identify on my own. The topics presented each week at the grief group brought those emotions to the surface where I could stand back and see them. I snagged some of them and managed to squeeze the thoughts into words in a journal; I found that therapeutic.

Through the grief group, I met a roomful of other recent widows and was relieved to discover that I wasn't alone. We told our stories: the day it happened and the struggles since. We cried together, held onto deep silence together, and shared some precious moments, even laughing at our late husbands or at ourselves with a freedom we could find nowhere else. But those dear ladies were just as hurt and confused as I was, if not more. Some of them were angry, others sweetly claimed God's promises, and the rest scrambled to fill the void in their lives with activities ranging from Bible studies to boyfriends.

I enjoyed the group and gleaned much from it, but I began to realize that I wanted—that I needed—an experienced role model to show me the way through the valley of grief. I needed to know whether or not anyone else had experienced the tension and despair that could build between that cozy quilt of comfort and an abandoned, crying child with scraped knees. *Does anyone wrestle with my questions? Who else has survived this journey and can beckon me on?* Those were the questions I most needed answers to.

Even though God seemed distant and silent, even though he punched me off my swing, I didn't find myself angry. I'd been reasonably provided for, my church and family were so supportive, and I was so grateful that Bruce hadn't suffered. I had no energy for anger. Yet. I was shocked, indeed! I was confused and terribly, terribly hurt—my innocence stolen, but I wasn't angry. Yet. But then the day came when I decided to ask God what I should do with all my questions. Sure, God seemed silent, but maybe I hadn't been praying right. I'd make it official this time.

*Knock-knock.*

I heard no answer.

*Knock- knock!* "Dear God, please let me in," I begged as I sagged at the door.

Still nothing.

At that point, some tidbits of information came to me. A woman in my grief group tried to comfort me with Isaiah 54:5: "For your Maker is your husband." I wasn't impressed. Next, I discovered that nearly 700,000 women are widowed each year in the United States alone.[1]

I did the math and couldn't believe the realization that hit me: *Over 1,900 women a day are widowed in the U.S.—and add to that thousands and thousands of women worldwide, each and every day!*

I put together the two tidbits of information—Isaiah 54:5 and the number of widows. And then I shook my head at the numbers: *one Bible verse in Isaiah vs. thousands and thousands of widows.* It wasn't a good ratio, and that statistical evidence of inequity, neglect, and abandonment began a slow scald on my soul.

*Knock-knock.* "What kind of a husband are you? Only one little verse for all of us widows?" I hollered as I rattled the doorknob again. *Sure, Jesus fed 5,000 people with a loaf and two fish, but now he won't even answer the door!*

Now I was riled and I had every right to be! I felt I had a legitimate complaint and the statistical data to back it up. And, I reasoned, I was in good company; even the Psalms are loaded with accusations and laments against God. Now I knew why!

God's door remained closed, however. I put my ear to the door and listened, but inside his house, all was still. *Silence? Great.*

I kept knocking anyway. For two or three days I knocked and knocked! Just as I started to consider morphing from a wounded little girl into a hardened, hateful, hermit of a woman who would hoard jelly jars and cat food cans, an utterly different thought—small as a mustard seed—was lobbed into my brain: *I'd been wrong.*

*Wrong? Me? I hate that! How could that happen? Did I forget something?*

Yes, I had forgotten. All of a sudden I remembered there's more than one verse in the Bible for widows. There's an entire book about us! The book of Ruth tells about three widows, and I'd heard the story plenty of times. Ruth meets her redeemer: Boaz represents Christ, while Ruth represents the believer. It's a lovely allegory, and that was exactly why I hadn't looked at it. A mushy love story; I sure didn't want to torture myself with a love story! *But what if it also contains direction for a widow? After all, what other book of the Bible is solely about widows? Has anyone ever looked at Ruth from a widow's perspective? What would happen if a widow were to read Ruth to learn about God's direction for widows?* Curiosity trumped anger, or maybe anger fueled my curiosity, looking for more to complain about. In any case, I decided to answer those questions. I'd have to read Ruth—again, and with a whole new set of eyes, tinted by what had happened to my husband and in my life.

So I did. I read it once, then twice, then over and over. I went to my church and dusted off the old commentaries lining the shelves of an unused room, a makeshift library. My anger dissolved and gave way to fascination. I clicked my way through threads on the Internet. I became obsessed. Like putting a puzzle together, I found pieces of information in Ruth that only a widow would recognize and appreciate—pieces that were key to the whole picture. Without fail, every time I read Ruth over the next two years, I was granted a fresh insight.

I asked every question—who, what, where, when, why and how—of every phrase, sometimes every word. Fascinating details of the history and the culture emerged. Ruth and Naomi became real people to me, like dear friends. I shared fellowship in their suffering through my observation and study of God's Word.

God had an extraordinary story for Ruth and Naomi to play out, but they had no idea what he was up to. As far as they knew, they were nobodies—like me. Ruth only knew she wanted to follow Naomi; she would be one of Naomi's people, Naomi's God would be her God, and she followed Naomi like a disciple.

The one thing Naomi knew was that God Almighty had seemingly brought her hardship. She was sure God had turned against her and was punishing her. She must have she felt as if she'd been knocked off her swing, too at the very least. She was sure God had—and would—continue to take away from her all that she ever loved.

Still, as I looked at her life, Naomi did something amazing: she didn't allow feelings determine her faith. Those in-depth studies revealed to me how real faith turns to God even when it's hardest to do so, when life crashes in, when it's hard, when it's messy, and when it hurts. In spite of her pain and her dismay, Naomi did what faith required. Despite her grief and pain, she put one foot in front of the other and headed back home. Why? Because she'd heard that God—the God she was growing angry with—had visited his people, and she wanted to be where he was.

From Ruth and Naomi, lives so ordinary and so much like my own—devoid of obvious miracles and filled with God's silence instead—I learned the honest answers to my questions and the truth about the tension between my picture of comfort and my experience of abandonment. I had found my role models: one full of despair, the other full of determination, but both full of faith and strength.

Step by step, without any guarantees, those two women walked away from the burial grounds of their lost loves, heading toward God's land and God's people. Nothing could stop them. I was spellbound by their faith, their courage, their strength, and I had to follow along.

I now had more questions: *Will they find a cozy quilt of comfort and show me the same? Will following these remarkable women help me find my path through sorrow? Will they teach me how to unlock God's house, to know what to do, where to turn, where to start?*

I delved in; my questions were theirs, and their journey was mine. I saw that Naomi prayed for rest, so I began to pray for rest. She helped Ruth marry Boaz, and the character traits of Boaz taught me how to recognize my own Boaz, Tom Hardy, to whom I am now married and without whom I could have never written this book.

Still, nothing was as I expected. God had ordained a better plan than I could have ever imagined.

"For whatever was written in former days was written for our instruction, that through endurance and through the encouragement of the Scriptures we might have hope." (Romans 15:4)

*Hope.* God's word offered me hope—the thing I'd been gasping for like a drowning person gasps for air.

The book of Ruth was my life preserver, and I clutched and clung to it through a great storm. The story of Naomi and Ruth helped me make peace with my own story. The sea billows of sorrow calmed, I washed ashore with something far better than a cozy quilt of comfort. When life crashed in, when love was rolled away on a hospital gurney, when my walk with God was difficult and painful, the story of Naomi and Ruth gave me hope on my journey through grief. And, hand in hand with that hope came purpose. Not a reason that Bruce had died, mind you; but a reason I was left alive—a purpose to live.

I pray it will do the same for you.

# Section One
# Grieving

# Chapter One

## *When the Unthinkable Happens*

In the days when the judges ruled there was a famine in the land, and a man of Bethlehem in Judah went to sojourn in the country of Moab, he and his wife and his two sons. The name of the man was Elimelech and the name of his wife Naomi, and the names of his two sons were Mahlon and Chilion. They were Ephrathites from Bethlehem in Judah. They went into the country of Moab and remained there. (Ruth 1:1-2)

*Dear Mother,*

*We are halfway to Moab! Today we're at the springs of Engedi, and tomorrow we cross the sea. We're all so excited that we almost dance at the mention of it ...and run too! I can't keep up with the boys. They skitter like goats over the steep hills, out of our sight. Eli keeps calling, "Slow down! Get back here!" What an adventure!*

*Eli hurries too. He can't wait to sell his pottery and my linens to travelers and residents along the Kings Highway¹ in Moab. He's such a good provider.*

*I know I'll be happy as long as I have him and the boys to look after and love. We're so fortunate to escape the famine. I know, I know. We could have stayed and eked out a living alongside the rest of you, but Eli promises me that I'll soon be draped with gold bracelets and rings! As soon as the famine is over, we'll return, set for life. Won't that be wonderful, Mother?*

*Lovingly,*

*Naomi*

# When the Unthinkable Happens

Have you ever felt as excited and happy as Naomi? Perhaps you've reached the point of knowing your dedication, love, hard work, and smart decisions were about to pay off. Perhaps you, too, have stood at the doorway of what you thought was hope and opportunity.

But then it happened: Life exploded, and all your dreams dashed away like sparks in the wind. The door of opportunity swung open, but death and a dark gauntlet of grief were there, just waiting to slam it in your face.

A young mother frosted cupcakes while she listened for the familiar sound of a pickup truck rolling up their rural driveway, the welcome sound of her husband and son returning from softball practice. Instead, she heard the phone ring. After she answered, she raced out the door in such a panic that she knocked over a kitchen chair and didn't bother to pick it back up. The door slammed behind her.

For a retiree, her husband's stroke hit as they stood in line at the airport, waiting to board their flight to Hawaii, surrounded by all their children and grandchildren—the dream vacation turned nightmare.

For me, my pastor husband, Bruce, came home from the church office, excitedly told me about leading a new friend to Christ, gave me a hug full of promise, love, and desire, and then hurried through the door to go downstairs to exercise and lift weights. Bruce was later carried back upstairs on a stretcher, slid into an ambulance, and pronounced dead at the hospital. Weeks later, when I learned he had died of a brain aneurysm, I was still in shock.

The book of Ruth opens with a scene of Naomi before the door slams. She's at a threshold of promise, standing in that brief, happy place where threats are inconceivable. Have you been there too? If you have, you, like me, have much in common with her.

*Naomi and Her Husband Were Problem-Solvers*

Naomi and Elimelech (or Eli, as I imagine she fondly called him) were packing their bags and saying goodbye to hard times. Blissfully blind to the heartache ahead, they planned to leave Bethlehem and start new lives in Moab. Elimelech had devised a grand plan to protect them from famine. With great intention, he wanted to take care of his family; today, we'd call it avoiding bankruptcy and finding a job. He and Naomi had never anticipated the worst. They'd never looked at it as the wrong door. It was absolutely unthinkable that their plans could possibly detonate and throw Naomi into a downward spiral of unexpected suffering.

*Everybody Loved Naomi*

Naomi's name meant "pleasant one" or "my pleasant one."[2] Blessed with such a lovely and positive name from birth, she grew to live up to it! I believe she lit up every room she entered. Children did cartwheels to catch her eye, her smile, her greeting, or her hug.

Do you know a woman like that? If you do, jot down the name of this favorite friend, aunt, sister, mother, or celebrity:_____. Now, read that name over again, and think of that wonderful woman as Naomi. In this way, she can begin to take shape in your mind as we start with her on her journey.

Naomi was the embodiment of a big-hearted woman who loved people and loved life, but Naomi didn't wear a halo or a t-shirt emblazoned with "Super Saint" under her robe. Rather, she quietly followed her husband and tried to survive, dutifully raising her children in a culture similar to ours—a society where everyone did as he or she saw fit. (Judges 21:25). Naomi's life—her concerns, her love, her hopes, and perhaps even the gossip at the community well—was very much like our own.

*Naomi Felt Trapped and Struggled with Questions, Regret, and Anger*

After settling in Moab, the unthinkable *did* happen, and at least ten years rolled by without her being able to return to Bethlehem. (Ruth 1:4) Elimelech had died, followed by Naomi's sons.

"Why did we ever decide to leave? Why did God allow the famine? Why didn't God stop us from moving?" Naomi must have cried out, at least in her heart. Our own questions may echo the same painful and unanswerable, "Why, God? Why?"

"Mistake! Injustice! Unfair!" we blurt out in anger when death and suffering snatch away our happy expectations and the one we can't live without. "It makes no sense," we say, our faith shaken to its core. Or maybe there are no words: we can only scream or cry in agony and anger.

"God could have worked things out differently," is a cold, uncomfortable truth that we often consider while our anxious mind paces like an animal in a cage. Naomi, too, experienced this hard floor of grief.

## Naomi Suffered the Ache of Loneliness

Stranded in Moab as a widow, bereft of sons, and burdened with the responsibility of supporting two foreign daughters-in-law, Naomi's emptiness was bottomless. Her only surviving family was back in Bethlehem, and she lived in an era with no phones, no postal service, and no email linking her to her kin and the people of her land. She might as well have lived on the moon. I sometimes wonder if Naomi spent dark nights in her bed as I did: drawn up in a fetal curl while loneliness seeped from every pore, soaking the bedclothes, rolling out in waves across the floor, weighing down the air of my empty, echoing house. I'm sure Naomi could relate, for sorrow caught her unaware too, and she felt abandoned.

## Naomi Was Just Plain Ordinary

In the book of Ruth, God is rarely mentioned beyond prayers and blessings. Nevertheless, this record of ancient life is important and relatable, for it puts us in touch with simple, ordinary women. Unlike the rest of the Bible, God never appeared to the people mentioned within it. There were no angels, no dreams, no burning bushes. He never spoke to them and never commissioned them to change the world. Nobody was healed, no water was turned to wine, no storms were calmed, and no new commandments were proclaimed from a mountaintop.

Why, then, was Ruth written and included in the Bible? Pastors and theologians purport that it highlights the royal lineage of David and Jesus Christ, foreshadowing redemption and showing God's providence. I agree with the experts, but I also have to ask: Couldn't Ruth be included in our Bible for a simpler reason? Couldn't it possibly be there because God loves widows?

When we feel invisible or overlooked, Ruth glows like a neon sign pulsating across time, proclaiming, "God never forgets us, widows! We do matter!" The ordinary lives of Naomi and Ruth convey that God is in our midst, even when the unthinkable happens and we cannot see, hear, or feel him. God's providence, below the horizon we see at the moment, looms larger for us than we can ever imagine, just like it did for Naomi and Ruth.

## The Arena of Grief

Here, on the other side of the doorway, when life has blown apart and we've landed in this parched, hostile wilderness of grief, Hebrews 12:1 tells me we're running a race watched by a great cloud of witnesses:

> Therefore, since we are surrounded by so great a cloud of witnesses, let us also lay aside every weight, and sin which clings so closely, and let us run with endurance the race that is set before us.

A race was not what I expected. This jagged running path was not something I've ever wanted out of life. Some days I just can't run; I'm overcome, and the best I can do is stagger. Other days, I only crawl.

On such days, this truth cuts through the fog of my grief: Ordinary Naomi sits in that cloud of witnesses, and a heavenly grandstand surrounds me, in a sense. Who else is watching me? Certainly Jesus and maybe Bruce, along with other loved ones: my grandparents, my still-born nephew, my girlfriend Laura . . . and the list goes on of those who've gone before me.

I gasp for the finish line as I gasp for hope. I push on. I'm not alone. It's a strange comfort to realize that Naomi and Ruth didn't know the story of their race would be in the Bible. They just tried to survive. And now, centuries later, I feel I know them. We are connected: we're not alone; we're not unknown. God has provided us for each other.

Together on this marathon, we run for our lives. The track twists, turns, and changes unexpectedly. At certain points we trip and fall. But on the horizon, eternity stretches out, infinite and unexplored, our destiny and the home of our desires, our finish line. Along the path, like spectators along the course, Naomi, Ruth, Bruce—your loved ones and mine—urge us on.

God, too, is there. He watches. He urges.

He knew Naomi and Ruth. He wrote their story.

He knows you and me, and he's writing our story too. Whether you have entered this race as a young mother hearing that her husband would never return home again, a retiree who's dream vacation ended with a funeral, or like myself and thousands of other widows who have unwillingly been put on this path every day—the journey has begun.

Listen as you run, as you struggle and strain.

Do you hear the cheers from the heavenly grandstand?

Faintly, faintly they begin from afar.

*Please let me say how sorry I am for your loss. I'm sorry you've been knocked through grief's doorway to this marathon of sorrow.*

*And then let me say how glad I am that you've found this guide. As I introduce you to Naomi, full of despair, and Ruth, full of determination, you'll discover worthy role models and teammates. Their examples will not only point out the dangerous valleys and blind canyons of grief, but also the profound beauty and breathtaking meaning of eternity.*

*We're running a race! No, it's not by choice, but nevertheless we must run. Let this page mark the starting point of what will become your extraordinary path to hope and purpose.*

*Fill in the blanks on the following page for your own imaginary postcard, addressed to yourself, your loved one, or to God.*

Dear _____,

I'm pretty ordinary, like Naomi.

Here's what my life was like before my loss:

I lived in_____.

My family members were_____

_____

Some of my friends were _____

_____

My occupation was _____

_____

I went to church at _____

_____

People described me as _____

_____

The best way to describe my race is that I (circle one)

Run          Walk          Limp          Stagger          Crawl

I have no idea what the future will bring.

From,

_____

For whatever was written in former days was written for our instruction, that through endurance and through the encouragement of the Scriptures we might have hope. (Romans 15:4)

*Dear Lord,*

*Thank you for putting the story of an ordinary woman like Naomi in the Bible. Her story gives me hope because you authored it. You write each of our stories. You add the "extra" to the "ordinary"—extraordinary! Help me survive/run/win (circle one) this leg of my journey.*

*Amen.*

# Chapter Two

*Leaning into the Wind*

B ut Elimelech, the husband of Naomi, died, and she was left with her two sons. These took Moabite wives; the name of the one was Orpah and the name of the other Ruth. They lived there about ten years, and both Mahlon and Chilion died, so that the woman was left without her two sons and her husband. (Ruth 1:3-5)

*Oh, my darling Mother,*

*Are you still alive? Everyone else is dead! First, Elimelech. It seems like he only died yesterday, but it's been years now. Waves of grief still wash over me; I don't fight them anymore.*

*And now — how can I tell you? — my boys are...they're dead. Their caravan to Egypt was attacked.¹ Someone just brought me their ripped and bloodied robes. I hold these dirty tatters close to my chest and rock back and forth, back and forth. My sons, my babies, once filled these empty robes. Now they're gone, but I just can't...I can't seem to let go.*

*I can't bear it! I had such high hopes. My heart was so full and happy when we arrived. Then, when Mahlon and Kilion found their wonderful young brides, Ruth and Orpah... Even though I'd always wanted to come back to Bethlehem, I tried to be positive. I settled in to enjoy my beautiful family and blessed life here in Moab.*

*Now I have nothing — absolutely nothing.*

*Naomi*

# Leaning into the Wind

Three little words sum up what happened to Naomi: "She was left." This impartial news bit startled me with the shock, despair, and helplessness she must have felt. How could three little words be all that remained of her nurturing spirit, her love for her husband and sons? How could her life end up like that?

What's more, Naomi's mother, friends, neighbors, and everything familiar remained back in Bethlehem. She had followed her husband to a foreign country, and then she was left. Abandoned. Alone. Like a hurricane, this personal storm came through and blew everything away: Her friends and family from Bethlehem were gone, her husband died, her sons married foreigners, and then, her children died.

Scripture only listed her losses, but there were many ramifications.

*Naomi's Losses*

When Elimelech died, Naomi lost her status, safety, and place in society. Elimelech was her financial support; his life structured her own. An unmarried woman in ancient times was a person of little significance; an Israelite widow in politically volatile Moab was nothing more than a meaningless alien, particularly at risk for neglect and abuse.

After she was widowed, Naomi's sons married foreign women, a forbidden act in that time and culture, according to I Kings 11:1-2. Some commentaries suggest that her sons blatantly disobeyed God in doing so and their early deaths were God's judgment for that disobedience. Knowing God's law, what would Naomi have thought of the marriages? Did she experience the same heartbreak as parents do today when their children choose sinful lifestyles and betray the faith in which they were raised? To her credit, Naomi accepted and loved her daughters-in-law, but without her husband, she was likely forced to resign herself to never return to Bethlehem when the marriages occurred. Dreams of being back in Bethlehem, surrounded by her grandbabies, lifelong friends, and relatives were driven from her mind.

Finally, in a sweeping and final blast of loss, her sons' deaths blew away any remaining hope, security, and identity Naomi may have had.

The original Hebrew deleted Naomi's name in Ruth 1:3, referring to her only as "the woman."[2] Fitting, really, since that was all that was left of her. She could no longer claim her identity as a wife or mother. She was simply a nondescript woman, for those roles had been caught in the gale, only to tumble and shatter in the wind.

## The Many Facets of Loss

A year after my husband died, I found myself and my identity broken in many places too. The three little words "she was left" applied to me. In one fell swoop, I lost my dear friend, my parenting partner, my spiritual leader, and my lover. I lost my daily routine, which had consisted of scheduling everything around my husband. I lost my calling as a pastor's wife, and my dreams of grandparenting and growing old with my life-long mate were swept away like dust.

I could definitely identify with Naomi. I was left to raise our children and make important decisions alone. I was left without the comfort, security, and daily routine of marriage. I was left to face a future I had never signed up for. I understood why the original Hebrew left out Naomi's name, reducing her to "the woman." Half of me had been wheeled away on that hospital gurney along with Bruce, and now losses mounted up and threatened to erode away the rest. I secretly questioned my value and purpose. What good was I? Seeing Naomi's losses, and then realizing and listing my own was excruciating. I felt such a void; I felt so torn. Deep cuts were plowed into my soul, like a farmer turning the soil. But do you know what, dear reader? This deep pain of widows serves a greater purpose. It makes room for hope and joy to sprout, grow deep in our furrows, and transform our future. The pain of grief was cutting deep places in my soul for blessings I could not yet see.

## Lean into the Wind

A piece of advice I received the night of Bruce's death helped me square my shoulders for the winds of loss. After our trip to the hospital, my son Brad, my daughter Lisa, and I phoned my oldest daughter, Brooke, who was in her sophomore year at Moody Bible Institute in Chicago. We told her the bad news, heard her wails, and added our own. Then we gazed at each other, alternating between sobs, shock, and more phone calls as we sat on our green plaid sofa and waited for the clock to tick.

Outside our lamp-lit living room, the wind blew, and cold rain pounded and beaded down the windows, mirroring the tears which streamed down our faces. The doorbell rang a couple times, and one of us would let someone in who wanted to pray for us or extend their solemn sympathy.

When the doorbell rang a third time, I opened it to find Bob Sandham, an area pastor who had always been available to my church in times of trouble. Here he was again, ready to take on another storm. He stepped into our tiny front hall, refused to come in any further, and simply said, "I can only tell you one thing. Lean into the wind." And with that, he hugged me and left. His visit must have been less than two minutes, but those wise words became a mainstay.

Listing my losses was one way I "leaned into the wind." I don't know much about sailing, but the phrase immediately brought that picture to mind. If we want to go anywhere, the sails must be up and leaning into the wind.

*Make Your List*

When you feel you are ready to raise your own sails, write down some of the things you've lost in conjunction with your husband's death. Think of the ramifications. Go over the ways in which Naomi was affected by her loss of security, hope for the future, finances, and safety. Consider the losses I've discussed with you. Look at the ways I was affected by my husband's death—losing my friend, lover, and spiritual leader, my role as a pastor's wife, and my daily schedule. Have the winds of change blown away some of the same roles, security, and hope for you?

It's understandable if you can only think of external losses at first: "It's so painful to see that empty chair at the kitchen table" or "I miss having him in bed with me each night." Your mind is trying to adjust to a huge trauma, and details might be buried under an avalanche of emotions and shock. I encourage you not to think too hard. Just note what you observe and wonder why certain things catch your attention—like the empty chair or bed, the lawnmower, a basketball, bottle of aftershave or a tool belt; maybe a song, a vacation memory, or a favorite café. Eventually you'll recall what those statements or visuals really mean. The empty chair might signify the loss of companionship or disruption in your routine; the bed might be loss of your sexual relationship or even your restful, secure sleep. Recurring memories are significant as well; they might represent grief over the loss of retirement dreams and lifelong goals.

## Let Yourself Mourn

You are allowed to mourn each of these losses. These things were important parts of your identity. I think you should even grieve over unchosen celibacy. If you had lost your ability to walk, to see, to hear, to touch, etc., there would be a sense of sorrow and loss. The same should be acknowledged in losing your sexual partner and role. It's a valid physical impairment, and there is nothing wrong with mourning over its loss personally and discreetly.

God is fully aware of our losses. As in Naomi's case, this is the path he has ordained for us at this moment in time. His plan now goes beyond the plan he had for you as a wife in a married couple.

Naomi was left, I was left, and you have been left. We join millions of women throughout the ages and around the world. But, I know: that's little consolation. When we've lost someone we've loved so much, all other relationships fall short in comparison.

## Let Yourself Learn

How do we accept help and other people into our lives without diminishing the significance and loyalty of lifetime love? How can we get back to living with purpose and hope when the one we can't live without is gone? How will we ever experience joy and happiness without him? Like a sailing skill we've never been taught, we can be quite stymied and awkward about leaning into the wind. We learn this new mode of travel slowly, by trial and error and by sorting life into little lists and gatherings of days ticked off on the calendar.

In the days to come, we will realize comfort as we lean into this storm, catching each breeze and updraft. Instinct tells us to cover up, to hunker down and hide from the wind, which seems like more than we can bear at times. Instead, consider one strong gust—one loss—at a time. Open the sails, list the losses, and lean in with anticipation. Eventually, I assure you that the wind of God's Holy Spirit will fill those sails and move you along.

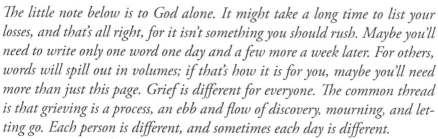

*The little note below is to God alone. It might take a long time to list your losses, and that's all right, for it isn't something you should rush. Maybe you'll need to write only one word one day and a few more a week later. For others, words will spill out in volumes; if that's how it is for you, maybe you'll need more than just this page. Grief is different for everyone. The common thread is that grieving is a process, an ebb and flow of discovery, mourning, and letting go. Each person is different, and sometimes each day is different.*

*At times, grief can be utterly overwhelming. Be kind to yourself and go at your own pace. Learn all you can about types of loss and all the diverse characteristics of grief. Attend a grief group, listen to recorded seminars on grief by Christian counselors, read books, or get counsel from your pastor, a hospital chaplain, or a grief counselor.*

*Don't brace yourself against this wind, for you cannot stop it or outrun it. Instead, lean into this storm! List your losses, mourn over them, and learn about this new phase of your life. Seek wise direction from people and sources you trust and ride out this storm. Comfort and hope await you.*

Dear God,

_____ is gone.

I have lost my best friend and so much more. God, this is my list of what I lost when I lost my husband:

B lessed are those who mourn, for they shall be comforted. (Matthew 5:4)

*Dear Lord,*

*I'm going to lean into the wind and grieve over my many losses. I'm going to mourn, for your Word assures me that mourners will be comforted. Help me learn all I can about navigating this new life. Eventually I know I will discover the wind of your Holy Spirit ministering to me.*

*Amen.*

# Chapter Three

## *Moving On*

Then she arose with her daughters-in-law to return from the country of Moab, for she had heard in the fields of Moab that the Lord had visited his people and given them food. So she set out from the place where she was with her two daughters-in-law, and they went on the way to return to the land of Judah. (Ruth 1:6-7)

Dear Mother,

Yes, I do get a little emotional at times. I don't know if you got my last note, but I'm a little embarrassed about it.

This is to tell you that I have a good reason to return. The news along the Kings Highway is that God has come to the aid of his people. My most reliable traders tell me there is food in Bethlehem — that the famine is over!

Since our original plan was to return when the famine ended, in honor of Elimelech, that is what I will do. I will carry out his wishes.

If I thought I had only a little bit longer to live, I'd just stay here. I'm not that lucky though; I am sure I have many more years. You remember how young I was when I had my babies, don't you? I may as well come back to Bethlehem. I miss you so much, and there's nothing left for me in Moab.

You must keep watch for my arrival. I'll need a place to stay. See? I'm still a practical thinker, just as you taught me!

With love,
Naomi

# Moving On

Naomi could list many losses: her house, her homeland, her husband, her sons, her security, and her future. Naomi was left, and she'd been left more than once. She was virtually abandoned and stranded in a strange land.

If I were her, I might have drowned in the tears of my own pity party, but not Naomi. Naomi changed her life by leaving her past behind. She took action; the passive phrase "the woman was left" in Ruth 1:5 changed to "she set out" by Ruth 1:7.

*She left? Yes! She did it! She left!* Those two words make me want to cheer! It was a huge accomplishment for "the woman!" When the time came for Naomi to move on, as it does for all women who have loved and lost, she did it.

The timing is different for each of us, but the point of change is a universal certainty. Even the animal world can provide us with this important lesson.

A few months after my husband died, I was driving along a highway and saw a Canadian goose standing at the side of the road. It was strange because they typically live around open lakes, not roadsides. Then I understood; I saw its mate, crushed and dead on the shoulder of the road. Canadian geese mate for life.

If you've lost your mate—or even if you're a reader who hasn't—perhaps you can feel for the goose. Like the goose at the side of the road, there's a time to be still, a time to sit and grieve and watch the body, a time to stay. To ignore that, to pretend it isn't necessary, is irreverent, if not absurd.

To stay too long, to wallow in grief to your own grave, is just as ill fitting. That's not what your husband would want for you, is it? Let me say this gently, it's not what God intends. Life stops for a time, but it will pick up again.

But how did Naomi know when it was time to move on? The verse between "the woman was left" and "she set out" provides the clues:

> Then she arose with her daughters-in-law to return from the country of Moab, for *she had heard* in the fields of Moab that *the Lord had visited* his people and given them food. (Ruth 1:6)

### Naomi Was Listening

Two things helped Naomi know it was time to move on. First, she listened, and when she did, good news about God caught her attention. She perked up. God had come to the aid of his people. We don't know if she had been patiently waiting to hear good news for many years or if it was the first time she'd lifted her head up enough to hear anything beyond her own pain.

### Naomi Wanted To Be Where God Was Working

Secondly, Naomi desired to be in the place of God's presence and blessing. When she heard that God had rescued Israel from the famine, her heart welcomed the call home and infused her with action. If God was back in Israel, that was where she wanted to be too. She would no longer run away from famine; it was time to run back to God. Returning to Bethlehem would be like moving into God's presence. Both her heart and her mind said, "It's time to move on."

### Naomi Prepared

There are things that must be done before a person can move on. Naomi had to prepare just as we do. Somehow, she'd survived in Moab for about ten years. (Ruth 1:4) There must have been a home that she'd have to leave behind, perhaps even a business venture such as weaving, pottery, or basket-making, with equipment, supplies, and inventory that she'd have to sell. Everything she owned had to go. The journey would be harsh, and all she could take was what she, herself, could carry.

I love the picture of taking only what she could carry. Most women I know try to carry too many loads, and we need that picture! When our survival depends on only what we can carry, it is much easier to decide on the really important things. That's especially pertinent when we have to close an estate full of memories, knickknacks, and trinkets and want to cling to them all!

Closing an estate takes time. If at all possible, this should not be rushed. Common wisdom says to wait at least a year before making the huge financial decisions required of widowhood. This may or may not be wise in your case. For example, if a widow cannot pay the mortgage on her home or the rent on her apartment, she needs to make some crucial decisions—perhaps quickly. Sometimes waiting entails huge costs, and not all widows can afford to wait.

But, whenever possible, take advantage of waiting. Feelings about the things we value swing up one day and down another. Knowing we have time can help us avoid letting other people pressure us to make our decisions. Waiting is better than regretting hasty, unnecessary choices. Seek wise counsel from a variety of experienced people and choose an excellent, professional financial advisor.

*Naomi Left the Burial Site*

Naomi left Moab, the burial place of her husband and sons. I wonder if it was difficult for her? I know that for me, moving was yet another degree of separation. I looked forward to my fresh new start, but my enthusiasm was bittersweet. Two years after I was remarried, we moved to Dayton, Ohio, some 200 miles from the cemetery where we'd buried Bruce. Physically leaving that last connection was painful, to say the least, but Jesus said, "Follow me, and let the dead bury their own dead." (Matthew 8:22 NIV) He didn't say those words callously or unkindly. It was simply his way of telling us we should live while we are alive. Life is for following him. His plan and purpose for us are about the kingdom of heaven, not dwelling at a graveside for the rest of life. Christ was no stranger to the human emotions involved with the loss of a loved one; he wept at the grave of his good friend Lazarus. He sees and understands our tears because he cried his own. He records them on a scroll, and someday he will wipe them all away (Psalm 56:8, Revelation 7:17).

*When Will You Move On?*

Ask yourself, "Am I ready to move on?" But please, before you hurry into an answer, know that the answer might not come until you start to prepare.

Don't be rash. Don't rush. Just start to get ready. Think about what moving on will require and how it will affect the other members of your family. Decide what possessions you can do without; note what stuff bogs you down rather than helps you out, and plan to get rid of some of the excess. Fix or paint small things in your house, weed your garden, start saving money, research places you might like to move to, and be sure to examine the costs of housing. Join a Bible study group to sharpen your mind and your spirit. Take vocational classes to learn new job skills and enhance your résumé.

Above all else, listen so you can hear when and where God has visited his people.

Remember, Naomi didn't see God, hear his voice, or feel the warmth of his presence. She simply had a listening ear and a ready heart. She paid attention to what God was doing and prepared to join in. First, she heard about God and made preparations to move to the place he was blessing. Next, she left the burial ground of her loved ones. That doesn't mean she forgot about her husband and sons; it only means it was her time to move on.

When I didn't see or feel God leading me, I remembered that Naomi didn't either. Nevertheless, his silence didn't stop her from seeking his presence. She desired to be where God was meeting the needs of his people. She was the exact sort of role model I needed.

*Fill in the points below when you are ready to move on. Think about Psalm 23:4 which says, "Even though I walk <u>through</u> the valley of the shadow of death." Grief is a valley to walk through, not a place to settle down.*

*This note will be like a trail marker. If you circle back a time or two, don't despair. Asking "Am I ready?" will help you get your bearings and keep you from getting too far off course. Make extra copies of this page now, before writing on it. In the months to come, you can fill it out again and gauge your progress.*

### Am I Ready to Move On?

*On a scale of 1 to 10, low to high, how ready am I for change?*

1    2    3    4    5    6    7    8    9    10

*Which of the following do I need in order to move on?*

*For myself (education, finances, health, organization skills, etc.):*

*For my home (cleaning, painting, gardening, repairs, etc.):*

*For my children or other family members I'm responsible for (communication, grief counseling, education, health, etc.):*

*Have I heard any news about God yet?*

*Have I seen God at work in any areas yet?*

Μy soul thirsts for God, for the living God. When can I go and meet with God? (Psalm 42:2 NIV)

*Dear Lord,*

*I'm still here, so you must have plans for me. Thank you for a role model like Naomi. I, too, will listen to hear where I can find you at work. Please help me to move on when the time is right.*

*Amen.*

# Chapter Four

*Mountains of Loneliness*

So she set out from the place where she was with her two daughters-in-law, and they went on the way to return to the land of Judah. (Ruth 1:7)

*Dear Elimelech,*

*I wish you were here.*

*My return to Bethlehem is very different from my departure. When I left ten years ago with you and the boys, we made for a small caravan!*

*Now, it's just Ruth, Orpah and I and the stuff we can carry: water jugs, dried figs, bread, one last raisin cake for each of us, and mantles to wrap up in at night. My walking stick, too; it's a bit of defense. Not much, but better than nothing against wild animals or robbers.*

*You shouldn't have left me.*

*I still love you.*

*Forever,*

*Naomi*

# Mountains of Loneliness

I had always assumed Naomi's walk back to Bethlehem to be something like a pleasurable Sunday afternoon stroll, maybe three hours or so. How wrong I was!

Of course, Naomi's commute was the furthest thing from my mind one morning in July as I sped my car east on I-90 from Ohio to Schroon Lake, New York. Brad was in the back seat with his friend Erik. I was taking them to Word of Life Island for a week of teen camp. While they were there, I would stay at the Word of Life Inn & Conference Center for adults, compliments of some very kind people.

It was a 500-mile trip on unfamiliar roads, so I made it a 2-day drive. We spent the night in Buffalo, and things were pretty routine: find the motel after a few frustrating wrong turns, see what the TV featured, learn what time the continental breakfast would be ready, peel the boys away from their videogames and chase them out to the pool where I knew they'd get some exercise and fun, and then watch a movie in the luxury of bed until sleep took over.

The next morning, we jammed the car back up with our suitcases, sleeping bags, pillows, and other accoutrements of the long car ride: maps, cell phone, candy and drinks in the front seat, boys and their electronic games in the back. The only empty place in the car was deep inside of me. With the boys wrapped up in their games and a long road ahead, I had plenty of time for pondering the thoughts, worries, and emotions swirling around in my head but avoiding the hole Bruce had left in my heart.

Although Bruce had died a year and a half prior, that was my first time to go anywhere by myself. Once I dropped the boys off for their ferry to the island, I'd be entirely on my own—no children, no relatives, no friends, and not even a roommate.

I found myself curious and apprehensive at the same time. *Will I find any single women to pal around with? What will I do if everyone else is married? Or, worse yet, what if there are single men there?* Apprehension began to win out.

After driving on the turnpike for several hours, I exited at Utica, New York. We bypassed the city, and when we crested a long hill, the Adirondacks rolled out in endless summertime greens of pine and maple covered mountain ranges before me. My breath caught as if I were at the top of a Ferris wheel. Beautiful, wide open wilderness filled the horizon. Somewhere in all those layers of mountains, further than I could see, was my destination. The road ahead was full of steep climbs, hairpin turns, and pristine forests. Emotions swelled inside my chest.

## Mountains of Loneliness and Abandonment

My throat tightened; it was more than a summer vacation. Those mountains symbolized my personal mountains of loneliness and feelings of abandonment. I had been praying since April for contentment, but it seemed like God had remained silent on the matter. I couldn't see my destination, my comfort, or any sort of future. I wasn't even sure if such things existed for a widow.

My oldest daughter, Brooke, had been married just days before. The wedding had been beautiful, and I was delighted with my new son-in-law. All the planning had gone well, but I was emotionally spent. Seeing the Adirondacks overwhelmed me.

I can't imagine how Naomi felt as she gazed from the plateau of Moab down to the peninsula of the Dead Sea she'd have to cross. Her view held little greenery and no fresh water along the barren shores of the Dead Sea and up the rugged switchbacks into the Judean wilderness. I wondered, *Did she feel as apprehensive as I do? Did she have personal mountains to cross too?*

## Mountains of Physical Challenge

Dr. Charles Dyer, Professor-at-Large at Moody Bible Institute and host of "The Land and the Book" radio program told me this about Naomi and Ruth's journey from Moab:

> *"The leg of the journey by the Dead Sea would have been very difficult. Between the eastern shore of the Dead Sea (as one left Moab)*

*and the base of the Judean Wilderness at Engedi, there was no drinkable water. Travelers would have needed to fill up their jars or waterskins and carry all the water they would need for the next four or five hours in the heat of the desert. For two poor women traveling alone, it meant they probably were able to carry little else with them . . .*

*My admiration for Ruth and Naomi only grows stronger as I realize how difficult their journey really was. It likely took them a day to walk from Moab down to the Dead Sea, a day to cross the Dead Sea and walk to Engedi, a day to climb from Engedi up into the wilderness of Judea, and another day to walk through the wilderness to Bethlehem. Four long, hard days having to carry food and water, four days of steep climbs over treacherous terrain, four days surviving in the area where David was forced to kill lions and bears as he watched over his sheep (I Samuel 17:34-36). They were two tough women!"[1]*

*The rugged terrain near the Dead Sea, where Naomi and Ruth most likely travelled. Photo courtesy of Todd Bolen, http://www.bibleplaces.com*

*Lessons from the Mountains*

My week in the Adirondacks was very different from the biblical widows' trek through the Judean wilderness. I drove through lush northern forests cut with sparkling, fresh streams; they had to walk through desert wasteland on the edge of a salt sea. I slept on a bed with clean sheets each night; they had to sleep under the stars on the hard ground and could have been killed by lions. My life was pampered and soft by comparison, but facing my mountains did make me stronger.

*Okay by Myself*

I discovered I was okay by myself. Older widows had told me that having an empty house after their husbands died had bothered them at first, but after a while, the place they'd once shared with their mates became their own little nest. It was a comfort, and they became content.

I had found single women to pal around with at the inn, but my own room there became my nest and solace. I transferred the idea to my bedroom when I got back home. I could sit on my bed, nestle my back against the pillows, and not always feel the absence of Bruce. My closed door, the golden lamplight, the quilted pink, beige, and soft green colors of my bedspread and the leather of my Bible served as a lining for my nest.

*Freedom*

I discovered a certain freedom when I was by myself. I could be my own best friend and do what I wanted, when I wanted. I don't suggest that I was looking to be some sort of selfish diva, but I realized there had been obligations and appointments involved with our marriage, as in any marriage. Now I had more time and more choices as to what to do with it. Now I even had the TV remote control!

*Individuality*

I began to discover myself as an individual. When I introduced myself to other people at the Word of Life Inn, which I had to do when I was sitting at a dinner table full of strangers, those introductions came without any attachments. I wasn't Bruce's wife, the pastor's wife, my children's mother, or someone's friend. I was just...me. People seemed to value and respond to me, much to my surprise.

*Saying "Goodbye"*

I also said goodbye to Bruce. He had died so suddenly that we'd never had a chance for even a quick farewell kiss. Toward the middle of the week, I bowed out of the scheduled activities. I took an entire morning and, using a rose-bordered pad of stationery and a whole box of Kleenex, I wrote a letter to him until I was drained and spent. I told him everything that had happened since he left: how each of the kids were doing, how pleased he would be about Brooke's marriage, and so on. It had been a year and a half since I'd last spoken to him, and there was a lot to catch up on. After many pages of scrawling ink, I concluded with this: "It was good to have been loved by you, Bruce. I loved you in my imperfect way and was privileged to have been your wife. I can't tell you how this has broken my heart. All I know is—I'm glad it did. No regrets. I love you still."

I'm pretty sure that as Naomi climbed through her mountains in the wilderness, she must have understood that God no longer held her accountable as the wife of Elimelech and mother of her sons. He now held her accountable, as he always had, for herself. It was time for her to claim that and say "goodbye" to her old identity. Each step she took distanced her from the past and brought her closer to her destiny.

*The Healing Begins*

After I wrote my goodbye to Bruce, almost at the very end of the week of relaxation, basking in the Bible teaching, great music, meeting new people, and the delight of delicious dinners that I didn't have to cook, and housekeeping that I didn't have to keep up with, God finally spoke to me.

I was innocently sitting by myself in the auditorium listening to the Bible teacher of the week, Charlie Dyer. Yes, the same Dr. Charles Dyer who later graciously replied to my question about Naomi and Ruth's journey. His topic that week seemed tailored specifically for me as he highlighted different Bible characters who struggled with suffering and doubting God. I was mildly interested and found good food for thought. But I still couldn't find resolution to my discontent and the wounded, abandoned feeling.

Then the page turned. As I opened my Bible, the sermon led to the tail end of Hebrews 13:5 where God spoke another truth I'd forgotten: "I will never leave you nor forsake you."

Despite my mind's picture of God and Bruce having a good time up in heaven and not caring a bit about leaving me, the real truth was right on the page: God would never do that! He was with me whether I felt his presence or not, whether I thought he answered the door when I knocked—or not. He promised he would never leave me. Those words became very clear to me and planted a kernel of truth deep in the darkness of my grief. Change didn't happen overnight, I wasn't automatically done with grief, but God's truth put a turn in my path and pointed me in the direction of hope. I'd have much more to learn, but this was the start.

That was what I found as I made my way through the mountains. I came to the realization that the loneliness and abandonment I felt were not my ultimate destiny; God was with me. My feelings of loneliness and abandonment were merely a leg of a journey that would make me solid, free, and strong.

*Is loneliness an overwhelming mountain for you too? Do you feel as abandoned as I did? This is a chance for you to be your own best friend. Consider these questions and listen to your heart's answers. Be honest with yourself. Set aside some time to write out your answers to these questions.*

*Am I okay with being alone? Why or why not?*

*What am I more free to do now that I'm by myself?*

*Can I introduce myself as just myself, or do I need to add details about my past—that I'm widowed, that I'm a mother, that I work—to feel valuable or identified?*

*How have I grown stronger because of this experience?*

*Have I said my goodbyes? If not, is that something I need to do? (Consider writing a letter to say "goodbye" to your husband if you never had the chance.)*

*What do I think of God's promise that he will never leave me or forsake me?*

It is God who arms me with strength and makes my way perfect. (Psalm 18:32 NKJV)

*Dear Lord,*

*May I look back on these days and see that you made me strong and this path is your good and perfect will for me. Please turn my path according to your truth and give me the strength to keep going.*

*Amen.*

# Chapter Five

*Two Needs of Every Widow*

B ut Naomi said to her two daughters-in-law, "Go, return each of you to her mother's house. May the Lord deal kindly with you, as you have dealt with the dead and with me. The Lord grant that you may find rest, each of you in the house of her husband!" Then she kissed them, and they lifted up their voices and wept. (Ruth 1:8-9)

*Dear Mother,*

*So many worries — I have to tell someone.*

*This trip back to Bethlehem — it's not fair to bring my Orpah and Ruth back with me. I know they will face remarks and gossip. I don't know if anyone will marry them. They'd be safer staying here in Moab.*

*Yet, if they don't come back with me — I love them so — I don't know how I can leave them. How can I bear losing them, too? And, can I survive the trip by myself? What if I get hurt and no one is around to help me?*

*My thoughts go back and forth, back and forth. If I leave them here I leave them to Chemosh' — the abominable idol of Moab — but they'd have an easier life. They'd have their mother and their mother's home. I'm just their mother-in-law, and I don't know if I have a home.*

*I don't know what to do. Should they come or shouldn't they?*

*I hate making these decisions by myself.*

*Naomi*

# Two Needs of Every Widow

Naomi struggled with something many of us face, widowed or not: fear of the future. Questions of doing right by Orpah and Ruth parried with those of moving on. She had thought through every angle of their journey, their arrival and survival in Bethlehem, and all the pros and cons of the move for each of them. She knew there'd be losses before they experienced any gains. The girls could get homesick, and even she would miss the Moabites who'd seen her through so many sorrows. Sleepless nights of ideas, scenarios, and worries nearly overran her until one day on a dusty road in Moab, we read the first words out of Naomi's mouth. In Ruth 1:8 she burst out in a harsh command to the ones she loved most: "Go, return each of you to her mother's house."

Orpah and Ruth were probably rendered speechless by their mother-in-law's demand, but before they could object, arguing, "We just got started! We've planned this for days! Don't tell us to go back now!" Naomi softened her dismissal. I imagine she held out her arms and drew in her daughters-in-law for an embrace. Love could not hide for long, and a prayer blossomed as she then began to bless them with the words of Ruth 1:8-9, "May the Lord deal kindly with you, as you have dealt with the dead and with me. The Lord grant that you may find rest, each of you in the house of her husband!"

Deep love, appreciation, and respect had bonded the women together. Saying "goodbye" would not have only broken that bond, but also shatter their hearts and dash their dreams. As their weeping echoes in our ears today, this scene illustrates what to do when we've run out of options: we pray. Naomi models some surprising directions in this brief encounter that point us to God's intended and extraordinary path for widows.

*Pray in Spite of Doubts*

Praying wasn't easy for Naomi. Like many modern-day widows, she certainly had doubts to overcome. *Why pray about things when God's just going to do what he wants to do?* was a question that was posed by 9/11 widow Jennifer Sands as she started her first new year without her husband.[2]

Like Jennifer, many widows can picture multiple ways God could have spared their husbands. They believe he's all powerful, but they doubt they can trust him anymore.

*Would a good God let me suffer like this?* Naomi likewise questioned. She called on the God of Israel, the God who kept his promises and covenants to her nation and to her. We must keep in mind, however, the context and historical era in which Naomi lived.

Naomi was alive during the time of the book of Judges. Israel, as a nation, had no ruler at that time. Their obedience to God would have prospered them as a nation, but they habitually strayed. Israel was caught in a cycle. They'd sin, God would judge and punish their sin. Then they'd repent and God would deliver them. Then they'd turn back to sin again and . . . God would judge them. Naomi, an innocent bystander, was swept into the tide of God's judgment when famine caused her and Elimelech to move to Moab. Her sufferings during the famine and her time in Moab were a personal consequence of national sin.

This is one of the most painful things about personal suffering. What's the reason for all the pain? At first glance, it may seem random, senseless, and undeserved. When people commit a crime and are sent to jail, they're reaping a consequence (in most cases), but when we suffer without knowing why, it seems utterly unfair and cruel. Like Naomi, we have doubts. Like her, we ask, "Would a good God sit back and allow this?" Those who follow Christ faithfully, only to suffer such trials, would naturally feel betrayed.

It is this seemingly unwarranted and undeserved suffering that causes many widows to give up on God. Online discussion groups, blogs, and Facebook statuses post rants every day. Anger and hurt flow like lava. People abandon church, they don't want to hear about God, and prayer is out of the question.

On Widows Connection website, author Miriam Neff posts this description about widows:

> *". . . we moved from the front row of church to the back row of church and then out the door. We moved from singing and serving to solitude and silent sobbing, and then on to find a*

*place we belong. Approximately 50% [of widows] leave the church they attended as a couple."³*

Yet, Naomi was different. She didn't run away from God or try to deny him. Instead, she headed toward his place of blessing and she prayed. Her focus on God was such a normal part of her daily conversation that we hardly recognize her prayer in this passage. What started out as dismissal orders to Orpah and Ruth turned upward into a prayer. Although Naomi struggled with questions and doubts of God's goodness in her suffering, she did not excuse herself from his sovereignty.

*Pray in Spite of Pressure*

*How can I even pray with so many pressures on my mind?* she might have wondered. The stress of grief can threaten to press us beyond our coping abilities. Daily duties of life don't take a vacation or a time-out when grief comes to visit. Grief is a refiner's fire that consumes everything but the bare and sometimes ugly bone of our character. Of course, Naomi faced different circumstances than we do. You might think life was simpler back then, with no traffic jams, cell phones, and stock market crashes, but wondering if you will ever eat another meal and if you will find a safe place to sleep at night is a crisis in any era! Naomi prayed in spite of the burdens she carried.

*Pray in Spite of Pain*

*But prayer is too hard during grief,* a widow might rationalize to herself. A phrase from the classic hymn "It Is Well with My Soul," written by Horatio Spafford in 1873, brings a true picture to mind: "...when sorrows like sea billows roll..." Some days, those waves tumble in relentlessly! When we're barely hanging on it seems impossible to pray! We're raw emotionally, and spiritually we feel wounded and powerless, as if our prayers are a waste of time, bouncing back unheard off of some invisible rubber ceiling. Intellectually, the fog can be thick. Words are buried too deep to surface, and any prayers we can muster may come out choked and halting.

Who would want to pray with that many doubts and obstacles to battle through? Who else, but Naomi? She had the integrity, courage, and commitment to pray anyway. In the rush of sermons and Bible studies on the book of Ruth, Naomi is often portrayed as bitter and angry. They gloss over her as easily as many churches overlook widows today, failing to realize the secret battles that rage. But Orpah and Ruth knew their mother-in-law was a woman of undying faith, even when those she loved died around her. That was why they followed her. We can follow her too. Like Naomi, just pray—in spite of everything.

*Pray for the Core Needs of Widows*

What should we pray for? It's surprising enough that Naomi prayed, but tucked in her prayer are requests for the richest gifts in the world: kindness and rest. Imagine a godly older woman putting a hand on your shoulder and uttering Ruth 1:8-9 over you:

"May the Lord deal *kindly* with you, as you have dealt with the dead and with me. The Lord grant that you may find *rest*, each of you in the house of her husband!" Aren't those two things—kindness and rest—what our widows' hearts most desire? We cannot magically summon or willfully acquire either one of these gifts. God's kindness births our survival and vigor. He alone provides the rest for which our souls yearn. Naomi petitioned God for the good things she herself most desired. Her simple prayer cupped the essential needs of widows: kindness and rest.

*Kindness*

Could you use some kindness today? Death never arrives easily or at the right time. In the initial chaos of loss, widows can be overwhelmed with an avalanche of chores, important decisions, lifetime events.

Widows come in all ages, all circumstances. Youth is not an exclusion from widowhood. Nor is pregnancy, or a large family. I've met widows who were six-months pregnant with their first child when daddy died, and others who've had ten or twelve children, with many still at home. Death doesn't wait for the husband to have his estate in order or a life insurance policy in place. Oh, how these survivors could use a little kindness! No one knows the private pain and the darkness they face!

Seemingly successful business men pass away, and business partners turn into wolves, pressuring the widow to sign away profits she is due, deleting benefits, and cheating the widow in shameful ways. She needs kindness!

Business owners die in their prime, and the widow, with countless other burdens, is left to step in, and save it in order to save herself! When coming home to an empty house after a sixteen-hour workday, what does she need most of all? Kindness! Isn't that the cry of your heart, too?

*Rest*

Naomi's second request is also crucial for widows. For most people in our hyperactive society, there is no room for rest on the ever-growing to-do list. There aren't enough hours in the day for rest. In fact, in spite of the fact that rest is mandatory for all human beings, our very culture views it as counterproductive, a waste of time. Grief is exhausting, and we must have rest. We must be able to sit, collect ourselves, and be still now and then.

The Hebrew root of the phrase "find rest" in Naomi's prayer meant "to settle down after movement or wandering."[4] It painted a picture of the end of a hard journey, a homecoming after war. Rest settles questions and soul hunger; it means satisfaction and contentment—a place to belong.

Can it also be akin to the relief that a widow or other caretaker might feel after losing the battle with cancer, diabetes, COPD, or many other slowly debilitating diseases? Many have told me what a mixed bag of relief and guilt they deal with after the death of their loved one. In granting rest, I believe God gives permission to accept that relief without feeling guilty. Relief is a form of rest.

Widows naturally seek this biblical definition of rest! Did you catch the little phrase tucked in the quote from the Widow Connection website? "… We moved from singing and serving to solitude and silent sobbing, and then on to find a place we belong."[5] The ancient Naomi brilliantly chose a blessing so fitting for restless widows, one that has lasted throughout the centuries and into today.

Like Naomi, let's pray, no matter how ragged and worn down we are from coping with all the doubts and obstacles. In spite of a suffering, broken heart, let's acknowledge God as our personal God who keeps his promises and covenants. Then, pray for the two core needs of widows: kindness and rest.

Sometimes miracles will be the answers to prayer. More often, though, it's a miracle that we pray. Believe it or not, though, God can and will use those overlooked, choked, and threadbare prayers whispered when we have no options to light the fuse for a long line of oncoming events.

*Volumes more could be said about prayer, and you could read hundreds of books on the subject. More importantly, though, just pray! Faith is most active when prayers seem worn out and futile because then, you truly will be praying in faith.*

*Use the prayer on the next page to simply ask God for kindness and rest. In your journal, note acts of kindness and rest already received. They have been gifts from the hand of God. Save room to write down future experiences, more gifts, of kindness and rest.*

Kindness and Rest in My Life

*Ways I have been shown kindness this past year:*

*Ways I have extended kindness to others:*

*Moments of rest, satisfaction, or contentment I've experienced:*

*Where I have felt most "at home" this past year:*

This is the confidence we have in approaching God; that if we ask anything according to his will, he hears us. (I John 5:14 NIV)

*Dear Lord,*

*I need to ask for myself the same thing that Naomi asked for Orpah and Ruth. Show kindness to me as I have shown to others and grant that I will find rest, a place to belong.*

*Amen*

# Section Two
# Changing

# Chapter Six

## *Choosing Light or Lies*

And they said to her, "No, we will return with you to your people." But Naomi said, "Turn back, my daughters; why will you go with me? Have I yet sons in my womb that they may become your husbands? Turn back, my daughters; go your way, for I am too old to have a husband. If I should say I have hope, even if I should have a husband this night and should bear sons, would you therefore wait till they were grown? Would you therefore refrain from marrying? No, my daughters, for it is exceedingly bitter to me for your sake that the hand of the Lord has gone out against me." (Ruth 1:10-13)

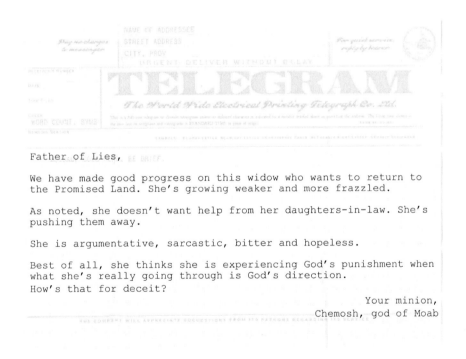

Father of Lies,

We have made good progress on this widow who wants to return to the Promised Land. She's growing weaker and more frazzled.

As noted, she doesn't want help from her daughters-in-law. She's pushing them away.

She is argumentative, sarcastic, bitter and hopeless.

Best of all, she thinks she is experiencing God's punishment when what she's really going through is God's direction.
How's that for deceit?

Your minion,
Chemosh, god of Moab

# Choosing Light or Lies

Naomi was tossed about, up and down, full of loving, wise prayer one minute and bitterness and sarcasm the next. Immediately after she prayed for kindness and rest for Ruth and Orpah, she began to argue. Isn't that so true in life? Just when we're at our best, our very next words threaten to undo all the good.

It was an emotional scene. Naomi's prayer and suggestion of remarriage had Orpah and Ruth in tears. They didn't want new husbands; they wanted to go with her. Naomi disagreed and barraged them with these sarcastic and argumentative questions:

*"Why would you come with me?"*

*"Am I going to have any more sons who could become your husbands?"*

*"Even if I had a husband tonight and then gave birth to sons, would you wait until they grew up? Would you remain unmarried for them?"*

The unspoken answers were cruel:

*"There's no reason to come with me."*

*"I have nothing to give you."*

*"You're being ridiculous."*

She was pushing them away, and her final exclamation was the ultimate shove.

*"The Lord's hand has gone out against me!"*

Naomi truly believed God had attacked her as his enemy.[1] The evidence grew monstrous in her mind and overwhelmed her: nothing she tried ever turned out right, and everything she touched seemed to die. She probably wondered, *Don't Ruth and Orpah see that too?* The famine had chased her away from her home in Bethlehem, and now she had to leave Moab behind. She counted off the losses on her fingers: her husband, her sons, and the life she had shared with them, not to mention all the practical, material things that she lost as a result—her home, equipment, and maybe even livestock . . . She was doomed, and she was certain that Orpah and Ruth would be doomed if they followed her.

Naomi wasn't the only person in the Bible to battle such thoughts.

"You have taken me up and thrown me aside," the writer accuses in the last half of Psalm 102:10 (NIV). In another example David cried, "Look to the right and see: there is none who takes notice of me; no refuge remains to me; no one cares for my soul." (Psalm 142:4)

Sound familiar? Have you ever felt like God doesn't care?

Up to that point, Naomi had been a strong and buoyant woman. Naomi was like Job when God commended him to Satan: "He still holds fast his integrity, although you incited me against him to destroy him without reason." (Job 2:3) Naomi, too, kept her integrity. But now, after years of loss, she faced a real crisis in her faith. The spotlight of God's Word exposed her in that dark moment as the sarcastic questions tinged with bitterness rolled out of her mouth.

A pastor I heard, speaking of despair and depression said, "When you get downcast and it's dark, remember what you learned in the light."[2] Naomi was downcast, but her prayer proved that she remembered what she had learned in the light. She had wisely asked God for kindness and rest for Orpah and Ruth. She had faith, but unfortunately, she also accepted many lies about herself and about God, and those lies sucked all hope from her.

The trouble with Naomi is that she was simply human.

I can relate—I'm human too! After I was widowed a little over a year, I prayed for biblical contentment for several months. Like Paul said in Philippians 4:11 (NIV), I wanted to "be content whatever the circumstances." At the same time, however, I had this idea that God had abandoned me. I pictured God and Bruce having a good time up in heaven while I was knocked down, cast aside, and forgotten.

As days of unanswered prayer turned into weeks, and weeks melted into months, my spiritual life became mechanical. I felt empty and disconnected from God. There was no cozy quilt of comfort. I believed God had forgotten about me, that he'd turned his back, walked away with my husband, and left me stranded.

The apostle Paul said, "So I find this law at work: Although I want to do good, evil is right there with me." (Romans 7:21 NIV) That was exactly what I experienced—pray, pray, pray, yearn, yearn, yearn—but the picture of God knocking me down and walking off with Bruce always lingered in my mind. Maybe Naomi experienced the same. She was good. She prayed the best for her daughters-in-law, but then the ugly idea she had silently tried to squelch for so long finally burst and surfaced: "the hand of the Lord has gone out against me." (Ruth 1:13) Bitterness, sarcasm, and despair flooded in and hope flushed out.

Here are a few lies it's easy to accept when we're suffering, especially when we feel alone in our trials:

- *God is punishing me. It must be my fault my husband died.*

- *God loved my husband more than me.*

- *Everything I touch goes wrong.*

- *God has left me.*

- *God doesn't listen to my prayers.*

- *God is always too busy with other people when I need him.*

To weed these lies out of our hearts and minds, we need to confess them to God and then guard our mind against them. When they crop back up in our thoughts (which they will), we must capture them again and replace them with God's truth. It's a recurring battle at first, but there is a technique for winning:

Ask a trusted friend to hold you accountable for untrue thoughts and to speak God's truth to you. Sometimes we need to do more than read and meditate on Scripture; we also need to hear it—really *hear* it—from a trusted friend.

Tell your trusted friend to be ready when you say, "Speak God's truth to me."[3] Explain to her that those words are a cue to let her know you are spiritually parched and need her to put a cup of God's living water, the Word, to your lips. Look up the verses at the end of this chapter, write down the ones that are especially meaningful to you, and give her a copy of them. She can use those verses to minister to you. She can listen to what you are going through and discuss with you the ways of God and how Scripture can and does apply to your situation.

This is a spiritual battle, so be aware that you might feel worse before you feel better. You may be bombarded with negative thoughts and confusion at times, particularly in the beginning. Remember, "Your enemy the devil prowls around like a roaring lion looking for someone to devour." (I Peter 5:8 NIV). The devil is a predator. He's out to destroy you, and he cheats and fights dirty. He is without mercy and will kick you when you're down. Don't be surprised when life gets hard. Like a lion, the devil considers those who are hurt, bruised, weak, and grieving as easy prey.

Be wary, but don't be afraid. Battles are to be expected in the Christian life. Choose to remember the light you learned before this dark time. Take comfort in the fact that God—your God—has already won. There's a mystery too—a part we don't understand: God allows us to be strengthened and matured when we are empty. Emptiness is an opportunity to fill up with God's truth, choosing light over lies.

*This exercise counteracts some of the false ideas that are easily believed when we're in pain. Choose the lie (or lies) that you struggle with and look up the verse (or verses) from the Bible (NIV) to fill in the blanks. If you don't have the 2011 edition of the New International Version Bible, you can easily access it at www.BibleGateway.com.*

*Have a godly friend or counselor hold you accountable for these or other wrong ways of thinking that can trap you in despair. Tell them, "Speak God's truth to me."*

*Lie:* God is punishing me. It must be my fault my husband died.
*Truth:* "You intended to harm me but God intended it for _____ to accomplish what is now being done..." (Genesis 50:20 NIV)

*Lie:* God loved my husband more than me.
*Truth:* "I have loved _____ with an everlasting love..." (Jeremiah 31:3 NIV)

*Lie:* Everything I touch goes wrong.
*Truth:* "For in the day of trouble, he will keep __ safe in his dwelling; he will hide __ in the shelter of his sacred tent and set __ high upon a rock." (Psalm 27:5 NIV)

*Lie:* God has left me.
*Truth:* "The Lord himself goes before you and will be _____ you; he will _____ leave you ___ forsake you. Do not be afraid; do not be discouraged." (Deuteronomy 31:8 NIV)

*Lie:* God doesn't hear my prayers.
*Truth:* "I waited patiently for the Lord; he _____ to __ and _____ my cry." (Psalm 40:1 NIV)

*Lie:* God is too busy with other people when I need Him.
*Truth:* "The Lord is _____ to the brokenhearted and _____ those who are crushed in spirit." (Psalm 34:18 NIV)

My soul is weary with sorrow; strengthen me according to your word. (Psalm 119:28 NIV)


*Dear Lord,*

*I am human, just like Naomi. Please forgive me for my wrong thoughts. Continue to direct me, even though it's hard. Strengthen me with your truth. I am grateful for the truth of your Word, your forgiveness, and your love.*

*Amen.*

# Chapter Seven

## *Three Choices*

Then they lifted up their voices and wept again. And Orpah kissed her mother-in-law, but Ruth clung to her. And she said, "See, your sister-in-law has gone back to her people and to her gods; return after your sister-in-law." (Ruth 1:14-15)

*Dear Naomi,*

*I'm sorry I couldn't come to Beth-lehem with you. It broke my heart to watch you and Ruth walk away from me, but I just couldn't.*

*I arrived back at my mother's house right before dark. I cried most of the way home. When you told me you had no husband for me, I knew I couldn't go. I'm still young. I can have a life ahead of me here in Moab. Mother has already heard of men needing more wives or concubines.*

*I will be much safer, maybe even happy. I don't want any more changes or chances with foreigners. No more handsome Hebrews sweeping me off my feet, like Kilion did. I don't ever want to fall in love again.*

*Thank you for treating me like a daughter. I'll never forget you.*

*With Love,*
*Orpah*

# Three Choices

"Will you get married again, Mom?" one of my children asked the night before Bruce's funeral.

It startled me and caught me off guard. I hadn't thought that far ahead. Even if I had, romance and remarriage was of no interest to my already overloaded emotions. It was a question that would have to wait.

Questions don't wait though. It's against their nature. They're intrusive and rude; they clamor for answers, and they don't care if we're ready or not:

*"Which casket do you want?"*

*"Will that be cash or credit?*

*"How will you pay the bills?"*

*"Where are you going to live?"*

I was surprised to learn that the book of Ruth provided insight for that last one, "Where are you going to live?" The three widows of Ruth embodied classic paths that widows take after a loss:

- Orpah chose to remain with the familiar.

- Ruth chose to risk an entirely new life.

- Naomi chose to return to her roots.

Widows of today do the same—remain, risk, or return. Considering the three biblical widows and their choices helped me with some of my own decisions. I believe we can examine these three paths to help clarify choices when we feel pressured to answer clamoring questions.

## Orpah Remained with the Familiar

Orpah went back to her family, back to the familiar. She didn't want to deal with any more changes in her life. The Bible text does not condemn her for this, although many Bible teachers do. "A-ha!" they say. "She chose immediate comfort. She took the easy way out, and she chose idolatry." Naomi's statement about Orpah "going back to her people *and her gods*," provides them with all the evidence they need, and it's a good case.

But an important reality to factor in before imposing judgment on Orpah is that processing grief requires a huge emotional investment and individual timing. Everyone's experience is different. Even those within the same family can undergo entirely different grieving patterns. Naomi had the opportunity of living in Moab for ten years before she decided to leave, so let's allow some sympathy and extend some grace to Orpah.

Orpah did the safe and logical thing. By remaining in Moab, she knew she could avoid all the unknowns of Bethlehem, as well as the dangerous journey to get to that unfamiliar place. The chaos and tragedy caused by her husband's death would begin to subside. It made sense for her to stay. Moving on could have smacked Orpah with additional loss and confusion.

I empathized with Orpah's decision. I hoped the absence of Naomi and Ruth stirred in her an encounter with her Creator and true God. To this day, I hold out the hope of meeting her in heaven, but I realize I may not. Although I don't believe we need to pass judgment on Orpah, her choice should serve as a yellow traffic light for the rest of us. We need to look both ways and test our own decisions. Are they based on faith or on fear of more loss? Are we holding back, remaining with the familiar, simply out of fear of the unknown, or are we convinced staying put is God's will? Orpah made a humanly logical and reasonable choice. Was it the right one? We don't know. All we can say on this side of heaven is that her choice stands in deep contrast with Ruth's choice.

*Ruth Risked an Entirely New Life*

For the greater part of my life, Sunday School stories and Bible picture book impressions made Ruth appear too goody-goody for me. A quaint, Victorian picture of her was painted in my head: the feeble, elderly, bent Naomi leaned on Ruth's soft, lily-white hand as they strolled into Bethlehem on a gentle springtime afternoon.

It was quite a shock to get to know the real Ruth! She was a woman who had a hunger for God, compassion for her mother-in-law, and a generous dose of determination. Her faith was as great as Abraham's, and she gambled her life on it!

In a commentary on Ruth, Dr. Robert Hubbard writes, "Ruth's leap of faith even outdid Abraham's. She acted with no promise in hand, with no divine blessing pronounced, without spouse, possessions, or support- ing retinue. She gave up marriage to a man to devote herself to an old woman—and in a world dominated by men at that!"[1]

Ruth lived with passion and courage. She refused to spend her future sighing, "If only…"

While it was likely not a path she foresaw or would have chosen, Ruth realized widowhood was her chance at a new life. She could choose to remain in Moab or, like a disciple, follow Naomi and pursue the Al- mighty God. In choosing between Bethlehem and Moab, Ruth saw an opportunity to follow God. Orpah only saw change.

*Naomi Returned to Her Roots*

Naomi's decision was to go back home, back to her roots. She was a grim pragmatist in this passage. Backed into a corner with nowhere else to turn, she was emotionally distraught but determined. The news that God had visited his people and stopped the famine in her homeland gave her a glimmer of hope and a grain of faith as motivation.

Understand this: Naomi's faith functioned apart from her feelings. She didn't have the warm, fuzzy idea that God loved her and had a won- derful plan for her life. In fact, she seemed to feel quite the opposite: that God's hand was against her, punishing her; that everything she touched would be doomed; and that every turn she took would be blocked. But despite all the despair and negative ideas, Naomi determined to go back home, back to God, even if that meant dying along the difficult journey.

She had no expectations of comfort or rescue. She only knew God had come to the aid of his people. Her faith was not the subjective, spiri- tual, or intangible thing that we often label as faith. She had no visions or intuitions; God did not speak to her.

Naomi's faith was a physical activity. She had heard travel gossip, like rumors spreading through a truck stop, but she put one foot in front of the other, one step at a time, knowing that each step shortened the distance between her and the visitation of God in Bethlehem.

Naomi's heart told her God was against her, but Naomi's faith—a doing kind of faith—took her home.

Always remember your way back home. Sometimes we need to go back to our roots and let God use our family to care for us. I wonder if Naomi had to be stripped of all pride and self-sufficiency before she would return. Is that what it would take for some of us to return home?

Whether you remain in the land like Orpah, risk an entirely new life like Ruth, or return to your roots like Naomi, there is no safer place than God's will. As the three widows emulate, we can make different choices. God's will is different for each of us.

How do we know which choice is the one God wants for us?

Here are the factors to consider in choosing your path. His will is made plain by his Word, the circumstances he has placed us in, the counsel of godly people around us, the inner confidence he gives as we consider our various options, and the strength of our feet.

*Grief becomes more complicated by additional losses such as income, a home, other family relationships and friendships, routines, and lifelong hopes and dreams. Remember when you listed your losses at the end of Chapter 2? Sometimes circumstances do not allow us the luxury to remain until all these things are worked out. I know of widows who had to immediately put their house up for sale to make ends meet. In that case, the decision was made for them: They could not remain. They had no choice but to either risk or return and accept it as God's direction. If you do have the luxury of options, however, weigh them carefully. Seek wise counsel and don't rush or be impulsive.*

Consider the three paths:

- remaining where you are

- risking an entirely new life

- returning to your roots

Which appeals to you most and why? Which frightens you the most and why? Discuss with a friend, pastor, or counselor your motivations and how to discern the will of God.

List some pros and cons of relocating, even if you don't think you will. You don't need to have a place in mind where you would go in order to do this exercise. We never know what the future may hold. If an opportunity to leave ever comes knocking, having sorted your thoughts out ahead of time will prove invaluable.

Trust in the Lord with all your heart, and lean not on your own understanding; in all your ways acknowledge Him, and He shall direct your paths. (Proverbs 3:5-6 NKJV)

*Dear Lord,*

*Please reveal to me the path I should take. Do you want me to remain with the familiar, risk a new sort of life, or return to my roots? I trust you with all my heart. I praise you for your promise to direct my path. Help me acknowledge you and find the path of your will.*

*Amen.*

# Chapter Eight

### Faith Steps In

But Ruth said, "Do not urge me to leave you or to return from following you. For where you go I will go, and where you lodge I will lodge. Your people shall be my people, and your God my God. Where you die I will die, and there will I be buried. May the Lord do so to me and more also if anything but death parts me from you." And when Naomi saw that she was determined to go with her, she said no more. (Ruth 1:16-18)

*Dear Mother and Father,*

*Don't worry. Naomi did not kidnap me or force me to go to Bethlehem with her.*

*In fact, she was very hard-hearted and told me not to come. She scolded, she tried to shame me into leaving her—implying that I wanted a husband out of her. I finally told her plainly and firmly, "Stop. Not even death will separate us."*

*Please don't think ill of me. I mean no disrespect to you. Something inside of me urges me. I must find Naomi's God, the Almighty One! I saw the power he had over Naomi in Moab. He's not like our gods--manmade idols with no power outside their territory. This God—she can't get away from him! She says all her afflictions in Moab came from him, yet she seeks him. I'm amazed and intrigued.*

*Naomi's God has been speaking to her people for generations. He's the one who brought them like a flood out of Egypt. Remember the stories you told me of how Israel swarmed around Moab like locusts on their exodus from Egypt?*

*I think God is leading me out of Moab like he led Israel out of Egypt. So you see, I must follow.*

*I'll always be your daughter, but now I'm Naomi's daughter, too.*

*It's God's will, it's a risk I must take.*

*Love, Ruth*

# Faith Steps In

Ruth clung to Naomi as the solitary figure of Orpah vanished past the horizon.

"Go! Run and catch up with her," Naomi urged. "Look! Your sister-in-law is going back."

Naomi took a step back to separate them. Ruth lifted her head from Naomi's shoulder. Shifting her weight to her heel, she turned to the sweeping motion of Naomi's arm pointing to Orpah. As she did so, a sharp twinge rushed up her ankle. Ruth bent down and dislodged two small stones from under her right foot. They'd caught her by surprise, so tiny they shouldn't have hurt, but they had sharp, jagged edges. One was brown, the other was gray, and they were just ordinary, just two. But pain from their sharp points shot up her leg like Naomi's earlier prayer requests had pierced into her heart.

Ruth silently named them; one "Kindness," the other "Rest." She put them in her pocket and looked down the road where Naomi pointed.

The road was empty; Orpah was gone.

*Naomi's Faith*

Ruth then looked at Naomi, the pleasant and lovely one. In her, she saw the extreme pain of someone who had fought hard but was finally so beaten and trampled down that she could only say, "God is against me." She saw a Naomi without hope. Void of promise, Naomi offered Ruth no prospects, no possibilities, no future.

But in spite of that, Ruth saw something more. Was it determination, resolve, grit, spunk, or pigheaded foolishness? No! What Ruth saw in Naomi was undying, unconquerable faith. No matter what—whether Ruth and Orpah went with her or not—Naomi was determined to go back to God's territory. Her eyes constantly turned to Bethlehem like a compass needle pointing north. She would find her God.

Ruth's pagan religion had taught her that gods were territorial. For example, Chemosh, the god of Moab, only ruled over Moab and had no power outside its borders. Jehovah was God over Israel, and she was sure he should only rule over the area of Israel. A god's powers expired at the nation's borders, or so they thought and taught.

Naomi's God, however, crossed boundaries. He was even powerful in Moab. Naomi believed God had singled her out and attacked her in Moab, outside Israel's borders. God couldn't be contained or fenced in! Naomi's stories of the Almighty—his creation of the world in just seven days, Noah and the flood, Abraham, Isaac, Jacob, the Exodus—all stirred the wonder in pagan Ruth. She thought, *Wow! This Almighty God she speaks of is powerful in Israel, in Moab, and everywhere! Manmade territories mean nothing to him. The whole earth is his!*

Ruth was beginning to understand why Naomi had to go back to Bethlehem. Even though her family and lifelong dreams had been buried beneath Moab soil, Naomi saw a bigger picture, an Almighty God.

"God is against me," was what Naomi's bitter spirit expressed. But Naomi's faith took action, forcing her to put one foot in front of the other and carrying her back to Bethlehem. And how did she do it? One... step...at...a...time!

*Ruth's Faith*

Life suddenly became crystal clear for Ruth: she knew if she lost Naomi, she would lose her chance to meet and know that Almighty God her mother-in-law spoke of. In her sorrow she was learning to embrace life rather than avoid it, to live without fear today since tomorrow might be too late. Finding herself at a fork in the road, she fingered the pebbles in her pocket and declared her love for Naomi and a determination to experience her faith. Far from the good-girl picture I had in my mind, Ruth contradicted Naomi's command to "Go back" with a flat-out refusal.

"Where you go I will go, and where you lodge I will lodge," she insisted. The word she used for "lodge" was for life, not simply a hotel room.[1] Naomi's people would become Ruth's people; Naomi's God, Ruth's God. "Where you die I will die, and there I will be buried," she said, extending her commitment into eternity.

Naomi had honestly displayed that God was real in her life. He wasn't an idol; he was Almighty. He reached into Moab, sought after, found, and affected the singular and seemingly ordinary Naomi. This seismic tremor rocked the core of Ruth's pagan being.

When we begin to believe God is real, when we catch a glimpse of him as the great and present "Almighty," we will be driven to do the same as Ruth, forsaking all else to find him. God exists! We are shaken! The universe is not closed. God interacts with us. He intervenes in the affairs of mankind. He's as intimately acquainted with our existence as he was with Naomi and Ruth's. He designed our life and numbered our days.

For Ruth to stay in Moab would have been her loss. She saw Naomi's goodness and incredible faith beneath all that bitterness and pain. She knew the woman could pray and talk to God. Naomi held the key to eternal life, and Ruth chose to follow her to the death to gain it all. Ruth was ready to take a risk with a woman she loved and knew and trusted.

*Building Faith*

Widowhood blooms with such risks and opportunities. There's a tremendous freedom in being single, as well as many opportunities for personal development and growth. Columnist Andree Seu wrote while her husband hovered between life and death, "Now's a chance to build a muscular faith."[2]

Once we lose everything, we slowly raise our head from the rubble to find we've survived the worst. Of course we don't want to go through anything like it again; just the thought is near panic. But then again, it's almost a relief that it's finally happened. The shoe has dropped. A full and wonderful chapter of life is over, but a new page begins to open up; with eyes of faith we see that the constant factor throughout it all has been the sovereign hand of the Almighty God.

Has faith stepped into your walk to God? Has the fact that God has involved and inserted himself into your life caught you with its immensity? If you don't know how to understand God's will in your circumstances, even if you're angry with him about it, the first thing to do is what Ruth did. Lay aside that old life and follow after the Almighty. Step into the new. How? One...step...at...a...time.

*Watch for the woman whom God will send to be your walking partner or friend.* Even if she's only on the radio or in a book, determine to stick with someone who will lead you to God. Ruth and Naomi had each other; I believe God brings a variety of people into our lives at this express time. "When one leaves, another comes in," says my blogging friend Candy. Just as he provided Ruth with Naomi and Naomi with Ruth, he places people in your life too. You're not meant to go through this alone. Begin to look for those God has placed in your life.

*Immerse yourself in Scripture.* Read it and study it daily. Check it out several times a day! The Bible is your spiritual food, so don't starve yourself. Learn as much as you can from Bible teachers in your church, at conferences, on the airwaves, or in books, but never let those venues substitute for your own direct interaction with the Word of God.

*Seek many avenues of wise, biblical counsel.* Find another woman who can mentor you in following Christ and understanding God's will during widowhood. She may or may not be the same person as your walking partner. Find a women's prayer group, attend their meetings, and ask them to pray for you. Attend a grief support group in a local church in your area. If none of these resources are available, form your own group. A helpful website for finding or forming groups is www.griefshare.org.

Faith is something that is difficult to define until we see it at work. When we are at a fork in the road like Ruth and Naomi were, arguing whether to go forward or to go back, there are no signposts or heavenly traffic lights. But once we begin to move our feet, tiny pebbles of direction and seismic tremors occur in our soul. We are bolstered, and we can say to the Lord like Ruth said to Naomi, "Where you go, I will go." Faith is a good travel companion on this extraordinary path. We set our compass on the Promised Land, and a yearning for kindness and rest prods us along.

*Use the sketches below to note how much of yourself you see in Naomi and Ruth.*

Naomi: Trampled and beaten up by life, she thought God was punishing her. Still, she wanted to go back to the Promised Land because she had heard God was visiting his people with food. Like the prodigal son of the New Testament, she knew life would be better in her Father's house, even if only to get a decent meal. Maybe she even wanted to "tell God a thing or two."

*On a scale of 1-10, with 1 being "totally different" and 10 being "most similar," how much like Naomi are you in your relationship with God?*

1   2   3   4   5   6   7   8   9   1 0

Ruth: She also suffered loss, but where Naomi saw punishment, Ruth saw evidence of God's existence. She had never encountered the living God, and her response was as the person in the New Testament who found a pearl of great price and sold everything he had just to own it. (Matthew 13:45-46)

*On a scale of 1-10, with 1 being "totally different" and 10 being "most similar," how much like Ruth are you in your relationship with God?*

1   2   3   4   5   6   7   8   9   1 0

Whoever finds his life will lose it, and whoever loses his life for my sake will find it. (Matthew 10: 39)


*Dear God,*

*It certainly feels like I've lost my life, sometimes like I've lost my faith. Am I responding more like Ruth or more like Naomi? Thank you for loving them both and for loving me too, no matter what.*

*Amen*

# Chapter Nine

*Signs of a Good Friend*

So the two of them went on until they came to Bethlehem. And when they came to Bethlehem, the whole town was stirred because of them. And the women said, "Is this Naomi?" (Ruth 1:19)

*Dear Ruth & Naomi,*
  *I'm all mixed up.*
  *It's nice to be back with my mother—at times. Other times, she forgets I'm a grown woman and treats me like one of the children.*
  *My old friends are all married, busy with their husbands and babies. Maybe their busyness is just an excuse to avoid me? I wonder...Even my sister doesn't seem comfortable around me, and we were inseparable as little girls. Do you think she's afraid widowhood is contagious? Do I have a plague? Am I unclean?*
  *People surround me but I have no friends.*
  *At least you two have each other.*

*I miss you both.*
*Orpah*

# Signs of a Good Friend

When a husband dies, friendships change. I wish this weren't so because it's yet another rip in the fabric of an already wounded woman. What is so cutting is that we equate our friendships with personal value. For example, "I guess Carrie and Sean didn't really like me in the first place, or else they would have stuck around even though my husband's gone." Or maybe we suspect the other party: "Julie must feel really threatened and insecure about my friendship with Adam now that my husband's gone. I'm sure that's why she's avoiding me." Or, even worse, they suspect the widow of luring their man away!

This is a sore spot with countless widows. If you feel neglected and hurt by your old friends, you are not alone! Part of the problem is that our society does not know how to handle grief. They're afraid! Another part of the problem is that our society (and, often our church) does not know how to help single women. But at the very base of what happens with old friendships is simply a phenomenon of group dynamics. Friendships with other couples constitute a group. When one person of that group is removed, the entire group dynamic is changed. I'm sad to say it will never be the same again. It's nothing personal. It's not your fault or theirs. It's just the nature of group dynamics.

In the meantime, while we get bogged down with the mental and emotional gymnastics of misplaced judgments and the shape-shifting nature of group dynamics, we fail to understand and accept that during a time of grief, friendships become a revolving door. Old friends may leave, but new friends will arrive. If we only watch the exit door, we will fail to notice the new people coming through the entrance.

That was exactly what happened to Naomi. When she and Ruth arrived in Bethlehem, she announced, "I went away full, and the Lord brought me back empty." (Ruth 1:21). Picture it. Ruth was standing right beside her, had stuck by her every step of that fifty-mile hike, yet Naomi declared she had come back empty and that she had nothing to show for her life in Moab. Was Ruth invisible to Naomi and that crowd of onlookers?

Have you ever visited with someone who failed to introduce you

*81*

when other guests arrived? Awkward, isn't it? Maybe you're chatting with your friend when more people come through the door. They greet her and glance your way. She's so delighted to see them that she completely forgets about you, leaving you to stand there and wonder, *Did I just drop through the floor? Am I invisible?* It's like you don't even exist, and that hurts.

When Ruth declared to Naomi, "Don't urge me to leave you or return from following you. For where you go I will go," do you think she expected to be ignored and forgotten? No, but that was exactly what happened. After struggling for at least four days on a strenuous fifty-mile trek together through rugged wilderness, strict rationing of food and water, shivering through cold nights in the wild desert, and living on constant adrenaline alert for danger from men and wild animals, Ruth was simply brushed off.

Such a journey and commitment should have galvanized their relationship, bonding and making the friendship stronger, but hardly anything was mentioned of the journey, only Ruth 1:18, "And when Naomi saw that she was determined to go with her, she said no more."

I wonder, was Scripture silent about the journey because Naomi and Ruth were silent? Did icy silence and cold shoulders elbow between the two of them? Ruth had contradicted Naomi; the younger defied the elder. Did Naomi angrily stomp ahead and Ruth scurry after her, trying to catch up? "Wait!" cried Ruth, but Naomi swept her shawl around her shoulders and hurried on even faster. Was that how they traveled?

We don't know. All we know is what we might have done and the huge doubts that would have loomed in our own thoughts along the way: *Is this crazy? What if we get lost? What if one of us gets hurt? Will we have enough water? What about food? What if we're on the wrong road? Where will we stay when we get there? How will we fit in? Oh—why won't she just leave me alone!*

Although Naomi didn't want to admit it, she needed Ruth. Neither woman was in an ideal circumstance, and neither was there by an easy choice. They had been thrown together in Moab, and Ruth's example shows us what it takes to be a good friend even when friendships are in crisis.

*Ruth Was Available*

She was the sort of friend who would stick closer than a sister. When Naomi mentioned going back to Bethlehem, there was no hesitation, no second-guessing. Ruth was the sort of friend who, when called upon, would be on the next flight. She wouldn't screen her phone calls or text someone else while listening to you. If you needed her, she'd clear her schedule.

*Ruth Was Committed to Naomi*

In the stages of grief, committed friends are very important. They are proactive. They don't just say, "Call me or tell me if there's anything I can do." Instead, they give you something to look forward to. They invite you to lunch, they go on a walk with you, and call you just to talk and check on you. They might not be able to drop everything every time you need to talk, but they intentionally arrange to spend time with you.

When people ask what the best thing was that anyone did for me, I tell them about my sister-in-law, Kathy Bowman. For the first month or two after Bruce died, she called me every weekday morning. She didn't promise me she would and didn't ask me if I wanted her to; she just did it. Once I realized what she was doing, I looked forward to her calls. They were chatty and cheerful, just ordinary, and helped me remember what normal life was like. Committed companionship, someone you can depend on when life proves to be undependable, is a sign of a true friend.

A quick Facebook survey of widows I know revealed that the sheer number of people attending the funeral and calling hours was very meaningful to them. Also, personal and thoughtful gifts and tangible help were very significant, like visits to the cemetery, invitations to go out to eat, and offering to stay to eat that casserole with them instead of just dropping it off. All attempts to maintain friendship are very important to a widow.

*Ruth Was Acquainted with Grief*

She was a survivor, too, and Naomi respected her for that. We don't see her shocked, worried, or angered about Naomi and the things she said and did. She didn't get offended when Naomi failed in the introductions and told the village she'd come back empty. Perhaps they talked through some of the weirdness of grief, the roller coaster ups and downs, the unexpected joys, and the sudden cloudbursts of sorrow. It's wonderful to have a friend who has grieved well, someone to whom you can freely discuss mysteries and the afterlife.

## Ruth Had a Higher Priority in Life than Her Own Feelings

Most importantly, Ruth wanted to have the true God in her life, and in following Naomi, she was following after him. This enabled her to treat Naomi with grace, and she wasn't easily offended when overlooked. She didn't see herself as Naomi's savior, aide, or supporter, for only God could fulfill those roles. Ruth came alongside Naomi to accompany her on the journey back to God.

Friends who are acquainted with grief, those who will be available and committed to walk beside you on your journey, are gifts from above. And, like Ruth, young and foreign, they might be those whom we would least expect.

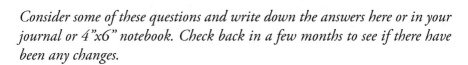

*Consider some of these questions and write down the answers here or in your journal or 4"x6" notebook. Check back in a few months to see if there have been any changes.*

*Are your friendships in a revolving door?*

*Who is exiting?*

*Have you allowed yourself to grieve these lost friendships and forgive these people for their flaws? Can you understand that losing these friends is more because of our societies' weaknesses and group dynamics than because of you?*

*Are you willing to allow new friends to enter your life?*

*If you were Naomi, how would you feel about having a much younger, foreign woman as your best friend?*

*Is there an older woman to whom you can be a friend like Ruth was to Naomi?*

*Write down the names of some acquaintances who might become close friends in the future.*

Two are better than one, because they have a good return for their labor: If either of them falls down, one can help the other up. But pity anyone who falls and has no one to help them up. (Ecclesiastes 4:9-10)

*Dear Lord,*

*Please open my eyes to see the friends I already have and the new ones you're sending my way. Thank you for each one of them. Also, please show me who needs me to be their friend.*

*Amen.*

# Chapter Ten

## *Brokenness*

She said to them, "Do not call me Naomi; call me Mara, for the Almighty has dealt very bitterly with me. I went away full, and the Lord has brought me back empty. Why call me Naomi, when the Lord has testified against me and the Almighty has brought calamity upon me?" So Naomi returned, and Ruth the Moabite her daughter-in-law with her, who returned from the country of Moab. And they came to Bethlehem at the beginning of barley harvest. (Ruth 1:20-22)

*Dear Orpah,*

*Ruth and I made it back to Bethlehem. It's good you returned to your mother's house like I told you to. Ruth was silly to come with me. I have nothing here. My land is gone: another claimed it because I've been gone so long. Even my dear mother is dead.*

*No one could believe it when they saw me. They hardly recognized me. "Can this be Naomi?" That was all that my old friends could say. Over and over they said that!*

*Well, how would they look after being on the road for fifty miles? Since my face has changed so badly I told them to change my name, too. "Don't call me Naomi—that name makes me sick. Just call me Bitterness."*

*I am empty. I have absolutely nothing. I hope you're better off than we are.*

*Mara*

# Brokenness

If Naomi's soul had a gauge on it like the gas gauge on a car, we would see that her needle had been on empty for way too long—so long that bitterness flooded in to fill the void. She was angry, distraught, discouraged, and dismayed because she believed God was against her. Hope was lost.

She had faith, and that was no small thing. Faith enabled her to put one foot in front of the other and keep going. But without hope, she felt hollow and lifeless inside.

She and Ruth made it back to Bethlehem after several days of picking their way along the Dead Sea step by step and climbing up into the Judean wilderness. They had carried all the possessions they could, along with water, food, and maybe an extra robe or an oil lamp for chilly nights in the desert.

Think of how we might feel after four or five days of hiking in the wilderness. Every muscle would ache, we'd be hungry, tired to the bone, crusted with dirt, and—to put it as delicately as possible—we'd stink. Naomi had been to the lowest place on solid earth. The Dead Sea is 1,300 feet below sea level! She'd also reached the deepest valley in her soul.

Naomi was so frazzled she had no tolerance for the Paparazzi-like welcome in Bethlehem. I imagine any children playing outside would have been the first to notice them—these two women materializing along the dusty approach to the village. The children ran to get their mothers, the mothers called to their friends and neighbors, the fathers and husbands came, and—well, you get the picture.

The town swarmed around Naomi and Ruth, crying out in disbelief at Naomi's return, unaware that an emotional volcano was about to erupt.

Like the townspeople, we may not associate bitterness, despair, or even depression with suffering. People hide what's inside. Our hearts can't empathize with what our eyes don't see; yet, unseen pain can be the greatest suffering of all. In the private soul, the loss of hope leaves its desolate, acidic taste. Naomi, physically exhausted and spiritually depleted, was raw. The henpecking welcome of the women stripped her of the pleasant, lovely, joyful carriage of her name.

I can almost envision them crowding around her, calling to each other, "Yes! I think it is Naomi! I thought she was dead! But no… It's her! She's back!"

They barraged her with questions and exclamations: "Naomi, what are you doing here? Where's your family? Who's this strange woman with you? Look at you! You don't look anything like yourself! What happened to you?"

Were there any welcoming arms or just a noisy crowd of curious busybodies, interrogating her at every breath?

In any case, Naomi was home. She'd reached her goal. As she was jostled through the crowd, though, her restraint wore thin. She stopped short, and the bitterness bubbling inside her burst out with accusations against God.

The original Hebrew text indicates that her statements crescendoed[1] to a finale that released the primeval howl and volume of her pain. (Ruth 1:20-21)

> *"Call me Mara, because the Almighty has dealt very bitterly with me."*

> *"I went away full, and the Lord has brought me back empty."*

> *"Why call me Naomi when the Lord has testified against me and the Almighty has brought calamity upon me?"*

She could have used Job's words from Job 16:12-14 (NIV): "All was well with me, but he shattered me; he seized me by the neck and crushed me. He has made me his target; his archers surround me. Without pity, he pierces my kidneys and spills my gall on the ground. Again and again he bursts upon me; he rushes at me like a warrior."

This is the worst of suffering: when God seemingly shatters us and turns away. Even worse, our Christian brothers and sisters seldom want to talk about this. Sometimes the loneliest place, the most painful place, is in a crowd of happy worshippers.[2]

A widow I called early in my experience told me that while her husband was dying of cancer, she knew she needed to go to church: She needed to worship, to be spiritually fed. Nevertheless, she was so drained that a single word, a single "How are you?" would have ripped and overwhelmed her.

The Spirit's work in her at that point was too deep to show obvious fruit. Her life was in a cold, harsh place—the season when death had made its approach, not the continual springtime of new life and hope which has become the Christian's expected game face.

She discussed this with her pastor and apologized for not attending. They came up with a surprising solution: She would arrive at church late and leave early so no one would see her. She'd sit in back with her hair undone, no makeup on her face, wearing her usual slept-in sweats and a frumpy t-shirt. Only the trusted ushers who silently watched over her knew she was there.

Still, it wasn't easy. Like Naomi, she had to embrace the pain and hang on when God's promises were not her real-time reality. Like Isaac, tied to the altar waiting for his father's knife to lay into him, she was also a living sacrifice, helpless to stop the knife of her husband's death.

We know so little of sacrifice. It's a "don't ask, don't' tell" sort of thing. It ruins our "God loves you and has a wonderful plan for your life" mentality. But I believe God wants this tabooed topic out in the open. It's okay to talk about it!

Why is it okay? Because this is what the Son of God went through. Let's face it: There are days when the unthinkable happens. Our eyes are held wide open to nightmares. The Bible itself is not all about fluffy sheep grazing in gentle pastures. It's about predators, evil, disease, and sin. And it's about a perfect Shepherd who took all of that upon himself for us, suffering the ultimate wrath of God displayed in a gory, excruciating crucifixion.

But, like my pastor, Cornelius Hancock, once preached, "The infinitely greater suffering for Jesus lay in his bearing sin and being separated from the Father."[3] Christ's most agonizing cry from the cross was, "My God, my God, why have you forsaken me?" (Matthew 27:46) His sacrifice went beyond the shedding of his blood; it also entailed separation from divine unity with his Father, whom he had known and loved since before the beginning of time. His death on the cross was not mere separation; rather, it was isolation and rejection from the holiness of God, and it meant experiencing the wrath of God for sins he did not even commit. He became sin for us. He was forsaken by God.

Forsaken, deserted, and abandoned. These all mean the same thing: the Father turned his back on the Son. Christ's words echo to us, along with Naomi's and Job's: "Why have you forsaken me?" My widowed friend experienced this as she sat alone in church; I felt it in my picture of the little girl knocked off the swing. We're afflicted, crushed, and abandoned, and we have to cry out *why*? Why have you left me?

Have you felt it too? It's a Christian's darkest hour, and it is truly akin to entering into the sufferings of Christ.

As Jesus endured the cross and carried our sin, he was torn and cast out from the divine Trinity, separated from the God he was one with. I often wonder if widows and widowers are the ones who might possibly catch a sliver of understanding the pain Christ experienced in his separation from the Father. The marriage covenant states, "they shall become one" (Genesis 2:24). When that union is destroyed at death, and death has parted us, it feels like being cut in half. We're no longer one with our mate. We're broken. Maybe, just maybe, that was a fraction of the sort of pain and separation when Jesus was forsaken by his Father. Maybe that is a part of the suffering of Christ we can now personally relate to.

We endure the emptiness, the onslaught of despair and hopelessness against our fragile shell of a soul. Without hope or love, faith alone holds us. It's not a sparkly, greeting card sort of faith either. It is a hard, intellectual, cold truth, a sharp stone in the walking shoe of our theology, uncomfortable and maddening.

Sometimes we want to get rid of that faith, to shake our fists at God and scream, but the evidence is indisputable: God exists, for creation proclaims his glory; Jesus intersected history, and he was crucified and rose from the dead as atonement for sin; Bible prophecies and promises have been proven and paid for with centuries of martyrs' blood; suffering is common to man, the legacy of Adam's sin; and weeping may last all night long, but joy comes in the morning. These are the facts of faith, solid rocks, unshaken by tears.

Like Naomi, the facts of faith descend on our words of despair. Night comes, and we cry ourselves to sleep. Jesus cried too. I think we understand a microscopic bit about how he felt forsaken by God. Is this what entering into the sufferings of Christ is all about?

But there is more: On the cross, Jesus blended the earthly and the eternal. He saw his mother, Mary, over whom Simeon had prophesied, "a sword will pierce through your own soul also." (Luke 2:35) Widowed, and without family at the cross, Mary watched her son die. Christ spoke to her and told his disciple to take care of her. In the middle of taking on the sins of the world, conquering them for all eternity, tortured and bleeding to death, Jesus Christ took the time to care about and look after a widow.[4]

The Son of God catches my breath. We do not have a God who is unable to sympathize with us; he cried out too. He cared for his widowed mother, even while he was nailed to a cross. Yet he does even more.

Naomi bled bitterness, but Jesus bled love. He didn't hold out to us a cozy quilt of comfort; he held out his arms as they were nailed to a cross for our sin.

I stand at a crossroads in my life. Shall I enter the sufferings of Christ and cry out in honest pain, "My God, my God, why have you forsaken me?" or shall I run in the opposite direction, denying my emptiness and embracing my anger. Shall I choose Christ or the inevitable bitterness of all else?

I can turn my back and walk away from the cross, but if I bend my knee and seek forgiveness and salvation, the gauge of my soul fills up red with Christ's cleansing, life-giving blood. I'm no longer on empty.

*In the early weeks of widowhood, music was especially painful for me. I literally choked on the words. Songs like "Great Is Thy Faithfulness" meant far more than I could physically express. But the songs of surrender and sacrifice were the hardest. As I listened to the singing in church on Sunday mornings I wondered—how could anyone turn such hard truths into pretty tunes and sing them without a care in the world?*

*You people have no idea what you're singing about, I thought. They were too young, too naïve, and they knew little of loss or suffering. They were mouthing the words, just playing a chorus, oblivious of the day they would need to make those very words their own.*

*When the psalms and hymns are not our experience, the repetition, memorization, and mouthing of them in music are our primer. They prepare us for days to come, hard days when we'll need to put them into practice. Spiritual songs suspend God's doctrine of personal surrender like medicine in an intravenous solution. They inject healing truth into the soul and help begin to fill the empty gauge.*

*Offer your singing as a sacrifice to God whether you're home alone or with a crowd in public worship. Thumb through an old hymnal or recall spiritual songs from the past. Contemporary Christian music, too, has come out with remarkable and touching songs which express doctrine we need.*

*Which songs and hymns have prepared you for this day? What true words do they inject into your soul? Talk to God about them and about his suffering and sacrifice for you.*

For as we share abundantly in Christ's sufferings, so through Christ we share abundantly in comfort too. (II Corinthians 1:5)

*Dear Heavenly Father,*

*Suffering has drained me. My soul is on empty, and bitterness is ready to pour in. I need you to fill me instead. Help me to surrender to your filling by seeking your forgiveness and salvation.*

*Amen.*

# Section Three
# Working

# Chapter Eleven

*How Will You Survive?*

Now Naomi had a relative of her husband's, a worthy man of the clan of Elimelech, whose name was Boaz. And Ruth the Moabite said to Naomi, "Let me go to the field and glean among the eas of grain after him in whose sight I shall find favor." And she said to her, "Go, my daughter." So she set out and went and gleaned in the field after the reapers, and she happened to come to the part of the field belonging to Boaz, who was of the clan of Elimelech. (Ruth 2:1-3)

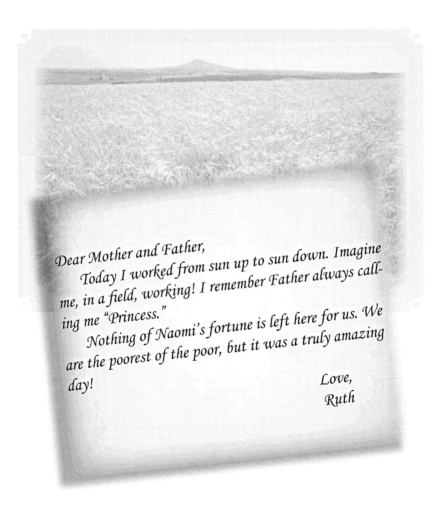

Dear Mother and Father,
Today I worked from sun up to sun down. Imagine me, in a field, working! I remember Father always calling me "Princess."
Nothing of Naomi's fortune is left here for us. We are the poorest of the poor, but it was a truly amazing day!

Love,
Ruth

# How Will You Survive?

My mouth dropped open with a gasp when I heard a pastor explain that a special offering would be earmarked for a widowed pastor's wife in Mexico: "She needs this money. It's not like here in the U.S., where widows are pretty well off with a big life insurance policy…"

Many people seem to think a widow's life insurance benefit is like winning the lottery jackpot!

They're clueless! Unfortunately, the stories of huge insurance policies far outweigh the reality. The truth is that most women are left with less when their husbands die.[1]

Why is that?

Do men think they'll never die?

The male mind remains a mystery to me, but I do know it's uncomfortable to consider how your family will survive without you. It's also difficult to buy insurance when there's simply no room in the current budget for another expense. The choices for life insurance can be confusing and frustrating. Buying life insurance is almost as much fun as filing taxes!

The result? A husband's death can plunge his widow into unprecedented financial disaster. Even when there is an adequate life insurance benefit, she could be in a real pinch. The insurance agent doesn't arrive at the funeral with the check. There's the death certificate to wait for, and that might have to wait for the autopsy report. Then there's transfer of funds, and so on and so on through the mountains of red tape before a widow sees any benefits at all.

Days turn into weeks. The funeral home, legal death notices, and the cemetery require payment at time of service. House payments and utility bills threaten to mount up. Assets are frozen in probate, and cash flow dwindles to a trickle. A memorial fund sounds noble, but when it's earmarked, it may not help meet immediate needs. Circumstances differ from widow to widow.

That's yet another reason why Naomi and Ruth are perfect role models for widows. When you have nothing, you have nothing, no matter what time period or culture you live in. Among the poorest of the poor, they had to start over. Where could they possibly begin?

Well-known missionary Elisabeth Elliott, widowed two times herself, offered this resounding advice throughout her ministry to people trying to figure out God's will for their lives: "Do the next thing."[2]

We don't have to wait around for the entire map of our life to unfold before we make our first move. Just do the next thing. The actions Naomi and Ruth took in Ruth 2 represented that advice. Their needs drove them to seek God's mercy, trusting in him to routinely meet those needs. Then, within the daily routine of meeting those needs, God's marvelous plan started to brighten on their horizon.

## Naomi Recognized Her Need for Recovery

Naomi was very quiet at this point. Not only had she been through the lowest point of land in the world, the Dead Sea, and hiked over fifty miles in only a few days, but she'd also reached her lowest point spiritually and emotionally. Her bitter and angry outburst against God drained her reserves until she hadn't a drop of energy left. I believe she took time to recover. If we need rest, we should rest; it's all right to hole up. We don't have to wear the Super Widow game face! Don't fake it till you make it! Fakery does nothing but prolongs and adds to grief. The physical toll of grief is surprising; physical rest is mandatory. We cannot deny this. Let the body have a chance to recover naturally through rest before resorting to medications.

In spite of exhaustion, Naomi did speak. Her four little words, "Go ahead, my daughter," revealed the gracious core of her character. She granted Ruth an equal dose of freedom ("go ahead") and affection ("my daughter"). Naomi's recovery didn't require Ruth to attend to her moment by moment. She's didn't cling or smother. Instead, she treated both herself and Ruth as mature adults.

During that intentional recovery time, Naomi refused to get caught up in worries about what they'd eat, how they'd pay for everything, or who they'd find to help them. She focused on rest for herself and release for Ruth. She knew her needs, and she set boundaries for both her body and her worries.

*Ruth Recognized Her Resources*

Ruth didn't need physical rest like Naomi. She needed food! Somehow, she learned about gleaning as a way for poor people to get food. Perhaps Naomi explained it on their walk out of Moab. With the barley harvest just beginning, the timing of their arrival was perfect for their chance at survival.

Ruth recognized and accepted with humility that gleaning was God's provision for the poor. We can read about gleaning in Leviticus 19:9-10. Harvesters rounded the corners of their fields rather than cut them square and clean. Gleaners followed, gathering the leftover stalks from the ragged rows and uncut corners. This ingenious technique freed up the harvesters to work quickly, enabled the poor to profit by working for themselves, and allowed nothing go to waste.

Ruth stepped into Bethlehem society willing to do the next thing to meet her needs. She would work. When she said "after him in whose sight I shall find favor" (Ruth 2:2), she showed evidence of thought and prayer in her decision. Finding favor would be like a sign from God to her and echoed Naomi's earlier prayer that they find kindness and rest.

Ruth depended on God's control over her circumstances and his leading her to the right field. Then she stepped out to glean because that was God's system of provision for her. In the big picture, she picked up what was left of her life and stepped into a field of opportunity.

Naomi's faith was shattered, while Ruth's was strengthened, but they coexisted and supported each other. They leaned on each other and learned from each other. They didn't compare or judge how far along the other was in the grief process. Stepping out to meet needs—picking up leftover stalks of barley like Ruth (essentially picking up what's left of our lives), or taking time off to rest and pick up some energy like Naomi—puts widows one step closer to that field of opportunity where needs will be met.

It's okay to be needy!

The tough thing is that when we meet disaster, we don't recognize needs as a blessing. It takes courage to face pressures and do the next thing rather than run away. Needs make us squirm and want to scream, but God wants us all to admit we're needy and that we can't make it on our own. Even David, the man after God's own heart, admitted his weakness. "As for me, I am poor and needy," he wrote in Psalm 40:17.

Such presumptions run against society today. Popular church cultures say that if we pray enough, if our faith is strong enough, or if we happen upon a form of worship that one way or another unleashes God's Spirit, almighty things will happen. Problems and needs will be cast off, we'll be blessed with health and wealth, and we'll find God's power at our fingertips.

Secular culture, too, has an unspoken rule: never let them see you cry. If we believe in ourselves, we can make it happen—or so we're told. Positive thinking, healthy self-esteem, and a dose of confidence give us the ability to change our life. A simple glance around the magazine-lined checkout at a grocery store lays the responsibilities of supernatural power on our shoulders: "Lose 10 Pounds Now…Organize Your House this Weekend…Fool-proof Ways to Make Him Love You…Save Thousands of Dollars…" and the list goes on.

Ruth didn't have to deal with the blame and guilt-building of such messages. Needs weren't a sign of weakness, defect, or helplessness in Bethlehem. In our culture, though, the thought of being needy is not comfortable; it's not considered normal. Anger, resentment, and envy over others' good fortune often lurk in the pool of needs.

But we need to recognize them for what they really are: Needs are doorways to opportunities. Just as God used Ruth's and Naomi's need for food to introduce them to Boaz, he uses our needs to move us in directions we would never selfishly choose. Needs motivate us to accept new people and places.

God doesn't force us to make painful changes. Instead, he nudges us with needs in order to make us willing to change.

We may be faced with many needs, complex decisions, and difficult choices. But for today, we must simply do the next thing—take care of the need in front of us. And tomorrow? Simply do the next thing again.

If you need to recover, then recover. If you need to start picking up the pieces of your shattered life, then pick up the one right in front of you first. In either case, whether you are lying in bed recovering or out looking for a job, watch for the field of opportunity in which you'll find favor.

*The Hope*

"The Message" Bible version puts Romans 8:14 like this: "This resurrection life you received from God is not a timid, grave-tending life. It's adventurously expectant, greeting God with a childlike 'What's next, Papa?' God's Spirit touches our spirits and confirms who we really are. We know who he is, and we know who we are: Father and children. And we know we are going to get what's coming to us—an unbelievable inheritance!"

Are we ready for so much hope?

Ruth and Naomi were. Their needs forced them to do the next thing. As a result, God had a field of favor and opportunity waiting for them!

## What Are Your Needs?

*Here are some needs and corresponding provisions. Take the first step—recognize your particular needs. And then circle the ones that seem to nip at your heels today.*

I'm weary. --- God gives strength. (Isaiah 40:29)

I'm lonely. --- God sets the lonely in families. (Psalm 68:6 NIV)

I'm poor. --- God is a refuge. (Isaiah 25:4)

I'm feeling low. --- God revives the spirit. (Isaiah 57:15)

I have unfinished business. --- God will carry it on. (Philippians 1:6)

I have many troubles. --- God will restore your life. (Psalm 71:20)

I'm insignificant. --- You will grow. (Isaiah 60:22)

I'm wounded. --- God will heal. (Hosea 6:1)

I'm brokenhearted. --- God is close. (Psalm 34:18)

## What Are Your Resources?

*Contact people and organizations that can help you. From people you know (individuals, family members, and your church) to those you don't yet know (government programs, grief groups, and financial and biblical counselors), there is a variety of help available. Also check out my blog at www.WidowsChristianPlace.com for links to various organizations.*

For he will deliver the needy who cry out, the afflicted who have no one to help. (Psalm 72:12)

*Dear Lord,*

*I honestly don't like these needs, but I know you can use them to situate me in a place of blessing. Like Ruth, please help me find a field in which I'll find favor.*

*Amen.*

# Chapter Twelve

## *A New Identity*

And behold, Boaz came from Bethlehem. And he said to the reapers, "The Lord be with you!" And they answered, "The Lord bless you." Then Boaz said to his young man who was in charge of the reapers, "Whose young woman is this?" And the servant who was in charge of the reapers answered, "She is the young Moabite woman, who came back with Naomi from the country of Moab. She said, 'Please let me glean and gather among the sheaves after the reapers.' So she came, and she has continued from early morning until now, except for a short rest."

Then Boaz said to Ruth, "Now, listen, my daughter, do not go to glean in another field or leave this one, but keep close to my young women. Let your eyes be on the field that they are reaping, and go after them. Have I not charged the young men not to touch you? And when you are thirsty, go to the vessels and drink what the young men have drawn." Then she fell on her face, bowing to the ground, and said to him, "Why have I found favor in your eyes, that you should take notice of me, since I am a foreigner?" (Ruth 2:4-10)

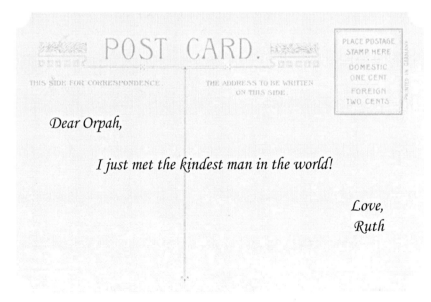

POST CARD.

PLACE POSTAGE STAMP HERE

DOMESTIC ONE CENT

FOREIGN TWO CENTS

THIS SIDE FOR CORRESPONDENCE.

THE ADDRESS TO BE WRITTEN ON THIS SIDE.

*Dear Orpah,*

*I just met the kindest man in the world!*

*Love,*
*Ruth*

## A New Identity

Where would you end up if you traveled as far as you could in the next five days? Would you still be in the United States? Maybe you'd arrive in Canada or Mexico. Or would you wake up on another continent, a little stiff from travel and from sleeping on a strange bed, grass mat, or in a hammock? Would you hear different bird songs in the morning, taste and smell unusual foods, and strain to understand different accents or languages?

Bethlehem, a walk of several days from Moab, was as foreign to Ruth as thousands of miles away from home would be for us. She allowed herself little time to acclimate though. Hunger must have popped her eyes open early that first morning. Perhaps she heard shepherds and goat herders leading their flocks to pasture, or maybe the village buzzed with preparations for the barley harvest: landowners calling out for one or two more hired hands, youngsters and teens shoving to get on the work crews, their memories of famine doubling the excitement of a harvest.

Gleaners eyed the landlords and their fields, looking for both sympathy and abundant crops. Ruth quickly joined the bustle, she needed to glean! She also understood her inferior position; in that foreign society, she was an outsider. It was crucial to find favor with a landlord and to find it soon.

She had to wonder how she'd choose the right field. As she looked over the barley fields surrounding Bethlehem, it was impossible to distinguish one owner's plot from another, for there were no fences! Land remained in the family for decades, so owners knew out of habit where their inherited tract ended and their neighbors' began. A bush or tree or perhaps a pile of stones served as surveyor's spikes or fence posts. Ruth fingered her two pebbles, Kindness and Rest, reminders of Naomi's prayer still in her pocket. Then she thrust herself into that patchwork of unknown boundaries and strange people.

I wonder if she went from field to field the way we trudge from employment office to employment office or website to website, filling out applications, getting a nod and a "Don't call us, we'll call you." As a foreigner, it's likely she encountered rejections, racial slurs, and weak dismissals: "Sorry, already filled."

Picture that ancient harvest. Men worked like machines, swinging sharp scythes along rows of barley. They'd grasp a handful of stalks in their left hand and cut them free with the scythe in their right as the air and the grain swished around them. The cut barley would stack up in the cradle of their left arm. Once that was full, they'd lay the stalks down, and the girls and female servants following behind would tie them into bundles of sheaves.

The men cut the barley, the women bundled it, and then came the gleaners. They grabbed the dropped or uncut stalks of barley missed by the harvesters or left along the edges and corners of the fields. Gleaners got the leftovers; they competed with the birds. Sometimes considered scavengers themselves, they could be driven off if they distracted, inconvenienced, or bothered the paid workers. Gleaners stayed out of the way. A good day for them would be in a field of sloppy harvesters who didn't bother picking up after themselves. Gleaning was about as profitable as collecting aluminum cans littered along the highway and cashing them in at a recycling center.[1]

"May I glean here?" Ruth might have asked, or maybe she just joined the crowd, hoping no one would notice. Scripture is silent regarding how she came upon Boaz's field. The author of Ruth sums up the Lord's leading like a coincidence in Ruth 2:3, simply stating, "she *happened* to come to the part of the field belonging to Boaz." Oh, that we were always aware of the *just happened to* times in our own lives! God was leading the widow Ruth, and he still does so for widows today.

Ruth found herself in the right place, but was it also the right time? She would have to test her boundaries to find out if that field would indeed bring about the favor she sought. Tucked between phrases of Scripture and rows of barley harvesters, we find her test—easily overlooked, but startling in context.

While gleaning that morning, Ruth had quickly computed that she and Naomi would need more grain than Boaz's expert harvesters were leaving behind. She had evidently found Boaz's foreman and had spoken to him about her problem. In Ruth 2:7, she asked the foreman if she could "gather among the sheaves." This was a rare and brave request, going way beyond the scraps of leftovers the gleaners usually picked up. Ruth wanted to reach right into the sheaves for handfuls of cut barley! The foreman didn't have the authority to grant such a wish, so he told her to wait for the boss. So when Boaz arrived upon the scene, Ruth and the foreman were waiting for him. Ruth stood before Boaz as he listened to the foreman and considered her fate.[2]

Let's drop in on their meeting. "Whose young woman is this?" Boaz asked his foreman, even though Ruth was right there. In a free Western culture like ours, we can only assume Boaz was looking for an introduction, but as a man in the ancient Middle East and a prestigious figure in Bethlehem, he would not look nor speak directly to a strange woman. His question presupposed she was someone's slave; she wasn't really a person to him. His question was more on par with, "Where did you find this new harvester?"

The foreman explained that Ruth was the Moabite who came with Naomi. He then stated her courageous request.

As Ruth listened to the men talk, her heart must have pounded. Was her bold request a newcomer's social blunder, a rude interruption? She must have wondered, *Did I make a mistake? Should I have kept my big mouth shut? I don't know these people! Will Boaz agree, or will he be insulted and angered?*

Boaz held the power to drive her away, to punish her, and to convince the whole village to ostracize her. How dare she, a Moabite, have the audacity to make such a request? Ruth must have sickened at the thought of what that risk could have cost her and Naomi. *I might have ruined everything.*

Completely at his mercy, Ruth waited for Boaz to decide her future. At best, Boaz, this landowner of superior status, would give directions to the foreman, and the foreman would convey them to Ruth.

But instead, Boaz himself turned to the socially clumsy, outside-of-mercy, undeserving-of-grace, destitute, and in-need-of-redemption Ruth. Like the sun shining out from behind a cloud, he immediately brightened her day, "My daughter," he called her.

I doubt Ruth needed to hear any more than that. Those two words instantly connected them, and Ruth now belonged. A moment earlier, she hadn't been much more than a piece of farming equipment, and now she was family!

Boaz went on to tell her to stay with his workers and be protected, glean behind the women (not among the sheaves as she'd requested), and to drink whenever she was thirsty.[3]

Ruth was amazed and relieved at the generous welcome from Boaz. In utter shock and gratitude, she bowed her face to the ground before him and exclaimed, "Why have I found such favor in your sight?"

Why? Because Naomi's God, the Lord God Almighty, was in control! He had guided Ruth to that particular field and placed her in favor with the big-hearted, kind, considerate man—the man who would, in later days, become her kinsman-redeemer.

Similarly, this is what happens when we meet our Redeemer, the Lord Jesus Christ. We may intellectually believe in the Almighty God, but the day comes when God leads us to a field of opportunity and offers us a personal relationship in his family.

Do you find yourself in such a place today, with this page unexpectedly in your hand? Like Ruth came to Boaz with an outrageous request, we come to God with one as well: "Will you forgive my sin?" Or you may frame your words, as did a woman I heard speak once. Driving along in her car one day, her thoughts battling between her way and God's way, she'd finally had enough. She pulled the car over to the side of the road, turned off the engine, and cried out, "Lord, get rid of all this junk in my heart!"

There are any number of ways to humble oneself, confess our sins, and ask God's forgiveness and acceptance. Yes, there are many different ways we can say it, but there is only one result.

When we cry out to God for forgiveness, our Savior God turns to us just as Boaz did to Ruth. He gazes upon us, and even though we don't deserve it, he forgives and calls us "My daughter"—fully accepting us into his family. We've met our Redeemer.

Even though the terrain of grief feels like a foreign land thousands of miles from home, we're not foreign to God. He's been watching us, leading and guiding even when we've been oblivious and unaware of his hand. As it turns out, he'll lead us to fields of opportunity where we can humbly bow and exclaim to our heavenly Redeemer like Ruth cried out to her kinsman-redeemer, "Why have I found such favor in your eyes?"

*One of the trickiest aspects of widowhood is that in losing our husbands, we've also lost part of our identity. We're no longer a wife or soul mate. We can't check the "married" box on forms anymore. We have to ask for a table for one at restaurants, open our own pickle jars, plunge the toilet, mow the lawn, and pay for our own ticket at the movies. These little incidents constantly cause us to grope the lonely hole in our souls, like when a tooth or filling gets knocked out and our tongue continually checks the empty space.*

*We may feel as vulnerable and awkward as Ruth must have felt while waiting for Boaz's reaction to her question. But when we've become part of God's family, no matter how lonely we may feel, we're never really alone. We have lost part of our earthly identity, yes, but we are complete in Christ when he turns and calls us "Daughter."*

*Have you come to the point in your own life where you've become part of God's family? Do you know for certain that you have salvation? This is more than church membership, taking communion or getting baptized. This is a personal relationship with God that is crucial to your spiritual life and eternal security! Please talk to your pastor about this, or if you'd rather—contact me. I'd be honored to discuss this with you. Email me at WCplace@gmail. com to start the conversation.*

*Meditate on the two verses below and mark any words that resonate with you today. Thank God for showing you favor as you remember your identity in God's family. Ask God to deepen your understanding of who you are in Christ as you continue on your journey through widowhood.*

Consequently, you are no longer foreigners and strangers, but fellow citizens with God's people and also members of his household. (Ephesians 2:19 NIV)

See what great love the Father has lavished on us, that we should be called children of God!" (I John 3:1)

*Dear God,*

*With the bad things that have happened in my life, I see my need of you. Yet, like Ruth, I know I'm an outsider. I've got all this junk! I need the grace, mercy and forgiveness of Christ for my sin. Would you turn and call me your daughter? Would you grant me the favor of salvation? Thank you for leading me to this point today and for your lavish love and grace.*

*Amen.*

# Chapter Thirteen

*Mysterious Kindness*

So she gleaned in the field until evening. Then she beat out what she had gleaned, and it was about an ephah of barley. And she took it up and went into the city. Her mother-in-law saw what she had gleaned. She also brought out and gave her what food she had left over after being satisfied. And her mother-in-law said to her, "Where did you glean today? And where have you worked? Blessed be the man who took notice of you." So she told her mother-in-law with whom she had worked and said, "The man's name with whom I worked today is Boaz." (Ruth 2:17-19)

Dear Orpah,

Ruthie has gotten herself a job. She's gleaning — a form of welfare for poor people here in Bethlehem. Someone was extremely kind to us today — she brought home barley worth half a month's pay! We'll soon be able to do more than just pay the rent around here!

She also brought me a napkin full of delicious, freshly roasted barley. I don't believe I've ever enjoyed a simple meal so much.

I pray you find
kindness as well.

Lovingly,
Naomi

# Mysterious Kindness

The sweet smell of fresh cut barley rode a light thresher's breeze across Bethlehem as the sun slipped down the horizon. The huge orange ball pulled the warm harvest day with it and drew in a layer of calm evening shadows. Birds flew to their nests, and Ruth hurried back to her abode.

"Naomi, I'm home," she might have called out as she approached. She wondered if she'd find Naomi still in bed, exhausted and trying to recover from their journey. *Would bitterness still emanate from her as it had at their arrival? Had the homecoming affronted Naomi with new layers of unresolved grief?*

Not knowing what to expect, Ruth pulled out the pocketful of roasted barley she'd saved from lunch. The sack of her threshed barley lay heavily on one shoulder as she pressed the other to the door and walked into the house.

"I've brought you a surprise."

Naomi barely noticed the napkin of roasted barley as she incredulously eyed the twenty-nine pounds[1] of grain Ruth deposited on the rough table that had been left behind in Naomi's neglected house. Naomi's keen business-woman mind quickly computed its worth. If an average gleaner's wage back then was as profitable as a bagful of aluminum cans picked up along a highway today, Ruth had just brought home the grandest of any grand prize! She'd hit the jack-pot in the history of aluminum can recyclers!

Naomi forgot her stiff muscles and aching joints. She forgot the bitterness she'd spewed at the crowd of busybodies the day before when the village jostled to make room for her and Ruth.

Naomi cupped her hands around the bulging sack of barley over and over again, like a woman over her pregnant womb. *How many handfuls? Is it really a full ephah?* An ephah could hold almost six of our American gallons. Imagine bringing five or six gallons of milk home with you. Ruth had gleaned an amazing amount of grain, and what she brought home wasn't armfuls of barley sheaves; Ruth had threshed it down to the grain alone—pure grain amounting to half a month's pay![2]

Questions and exclamations tumbled out of Naomi's mouth and ricocheted off the walls around Ruth.

"Where did you glean today? Who's field were you in? Blessed be the man who took notice of you!"

Boaz's act of kindness zipped like an arrow to Naomi's heart, cracked the cocoon of her bitterness and anger, and the grateful "pleasant one," Naomi, spread her wings and soared.

Kindness marked a turning point in my life, too, and it opened my eyes to a possibility I had written off: marriage. I had refused to even think about remarriage. My goal was to never feel the pain of losing a husband again.

The summer I drove to a vacation at Word of Life Inn in the Adirondack Mountains, a kind remark from a stranger changed my outlook. I mentioned in Chapter 4 that I had spent the night in Buffalo, New York. It was my first time staying in a hotel as a single parent—worse yet, a single mother of a teenage boy. In other words, I was a mom whose son didn't want to be seen with her. I had always enjoyed the companionship of my kids, but with fourteen-year-old Brad and his friend Erik, I was merely the chauffeur. The days of singing in the car, road trip games, and childhood chats were over.

We arrived at our hotel after supper. The evening was short and uneventful: taking away the videogames and scooting the boys to the pool was as exciting as it got. The next morning, I woke up before Brad and Erik, got dressed, and went to the lobby for a leisurely continental breakfast—alone. My first challenge was finding a place to sit. Little League teams in their baseball whites and colorful jerseys had swarmed the buffet, and all the tables were filled.

Luckily—or perhaps *as it happened*—I spotted a harmless-looking middle-aged couple with one empty chair at their table, and I asked if I could join them.

Those friendly folks were from Louisville, Kentucky, and we found common ground in golf. I know nothing about golf, but I had a friend in Louisville who organized a golf benefit every year, and that couple had played in it. That led to a quick summary of our journeys. They were traveling to a family reunion, and I explained that I was recently widowed and had been given a free week at Word of Life. They were touched.

The couple finished eating shortly after I joined them, but they seemed to enjoy my company. They could have left long before Brad and Erik arrived, but they kindly stayed and then graciously rose upon seeing the boys straggle in and spot me.

We parted like pilgrims on our individual treks, a sense of divine appointment hanging over our parting. Perhaps the heaviness of that mark on time caused the man to take leave with these words to me: "May you find another one true love this week."

I saw a shadow of horror and embarrassment sweep over his wife's face as she put her hand on his arm to extricate him, but to me it was a fine, brotherly blessing. I didn't immediately embrace the hope as Naomi had hers, praising God and crediting him with provision and care. However, I tucked the kind remark away in my mind and pondered it.

*What if I really do meet someone? Can I bear to remarry?* I'd spent many months convincing myself that it would never be the case. My life was already planned. I had enrolled in graduate school. In six weeks I'd be listening to lectures and beginning a thesis. There was no time for romance. Once I got settled in a career, I would buy a cabin at a lake, complete with a wraparound deck and an in-ground swimming pool. My kids would grow, get married, and raise families, and my beautiful grandchildren would want to spend all their free time with me. Aside from that, my two cats, a fire in the fireplace, a glistening kitchen, and some good books were my vision of a cozy future.

During my week at Word of Life, I talked to God as I scanned the auditorium during the concerts and Bible teaching times. *Is my new true love here?* I secretly wondered, and then I silently pleaded, "Oh Lord, please—not any of these men! They're all married and obviously too well fed!" And, thank God, none of those men were "another one true love" for me.

Still, it was clear that my heart had turned, just like Naomi's. When we're cocooned in grief, a nudge of kindness might be the spark God uses to ignite the hope within.

My eyes then opened to many other acts of kindness I had received:

times when my girlfriends had called or visited me without waiting for an invitation, how our associate pastor had happened to arrive while the ambulance was still at our house when Bruce died, and many others.

I've since collected these kind acts the way some collect seashells, fossils, or butterflies. They are vessels of life's mystery—prophecy and blessing together in one.

*How has God's kindness taken shape in your life? You probably haven't had a sack of barley hoisted on your table like Naomi, but maybe you remember things like unexpected gifts and cards, compliments, offers of help, or words of advice. Grief can make us ultra-aware of beauty too: a robin's song, a dandelion blooming through a crack in a sidewalk, or the clear, innocent voice of a child. We may be surprised at the strong emotions we feel over such little things, but these are God's messages of kindness.*

*Jot down ways people have been kind to you. Start with the first thing that comes to mind. Memories might take you back to the funeral or the moment your husband died, but don't be afraid. It's healing to revisit those scenes as you are able. Think through the days and try to remember how kind people were. Write down the little things too—coincidences, dreams and unusual events. Create a collection through your favorite media like a scrapbook, collage, video, quilt, etc.*

*Don't you feel a little better and brighter already? That's the mysterious power of kindness; it opens us to gratitude and hope.*

I will praise you, O Lord my God, with all my heart; I will glorify your name forever. For great is your love toward me; you have delivered me from the depths, from the realm of the dead. (Psalm 86:12-13)

*Dear God,*

*I long to give you sincere praise and gratitude. Open my eyes to your great and immeasurable love for me expressed by mysterious kindness I've received. Help me recognize how you have delivered me from the depths of my sorrow.*

*Amen.*

# Chapter Fourteen

*Transforming Praise*

A nd Naomi said to her daughter-in-law, "May he be blessed by the Lord, whose kindness has not forsaken the living or the dead!" Naomi also said to her, "The man is a close relative of ours, one of our redeemers." (Ruth 2:20)

Dear Orpah

I feel like I'm waking up from a deep sleep in a night so cold that it numbed me. Now, it's as if the sun has started to warm me. Each finger aches and tingles, and then it spreads to my arms, meets at my chest, and goes up to my head and down to my feet. I'm coming alive again!

I think it all happened the other day when Ruthie brought home that huge sack of barley. The next day we had it weighed and it was just as I'd guessed — a full ephah! When I first saw it, so heavy our poor little table sagged under the weight, I blurted out that God hadn't stopped showing his kindness like I'd thought.

How could I have been so wrong? How could I have felt so abandoned and forsaken by God? In spite of my anger and bitterness towards him, he poured out this abundant blessing on me—on us.

I'll never cease to praise him—not ever, ever again.

God is good, and his mercy endures forever.

Love always,
Naomi

# Transforming Praise

Kindness cracked the cocoon of Naomi's bitterness, but it was Naomi's response of gratitude and praise that put the wind beneath her wings and helped her soar. She saw that the answer to her prayer over Ruth and Orpah for kindness and rest had landed back on her own head with divine generosity and lavish grace. Where she would have been grateful for one portion of daily bread, the Lord provided twenty-fold.

Naomi had worked hard to get to that place. Healthy grieving is hard, it's proactive, and it's a choice. You either head into it or you stall. Psalm 23:4 (NKJV), a very familiar passage for funerals and the grieving, says, "Yea, though I walk *through* the valley of the shadow of death…" *Through* it! There are no shortcuts or detours. Crying happens; the tears will come. Naomi walked through her grief all the way to Bethlehem. Taking one step at a time took her to where she needed to be.

Like Naomi, we have to walk through unwelcome changes, but we will also receive kindness from friends, neighbors, and even God-sent strangers along the way. God empowers their kindness to break through our pain and open us up to a hopeful future and unexplored possibilities.

The question is, once that pain is broken, will we see the same source of kindness Naomi saw?

When Ruth's silhouette filled the doorway of the house with a bulging sack of barley, Naomi immediately saw the grain as a gift from God. She didn't credit Ruth's hard work or good fortune. Rather, her gratitude climbed like a ladder from the abundance of grain, to the goodness of Boaz the landowner, all the way up to God himself.

The book of Ruth is so much like our common life. God clothes his kindness in common, everyday human beings—people with whom we're all too familiar. There may have been those whose faithful service we've overlooked, be they our pastor, friends who've called, acquaintances who have taken the time to pay their respects at our husband's funeral, or church ladies who've chipped in to cover many behind-the-scene details that needed to be taken care of. Each and every one of these actions are expressions of God's mercy and grace.

Ultimately, God instigates all goodness we receive. As James 1:17

says, "Every good gift and every perfect gift is from above, coming down from the Father of lights with whom there is no variation or shadow due to change." That Father of lights, God, is the one we must acknowledge. As Naomi praised God, her recognition of his kindness released the gratitude and thankfulness that were buried deep inside her, and they came spilling out in verbal praises and thanksgiving.

It's interesting to note that Naomi's praise occurred right in the middle of this story, like an apex, a continental divide. From there on out, her attitude of gratitude created a hinge for the rest of the story to swing on. Everything changed because praise changed Naomi's outlook. Psalm 50:23 says, "The one who offers thanksgiving as his sacrifice glorifies me; to one who orders his way rightly I will show the salvation of God!" Naomi was on the verge of a change for the better.

Ruth's kindness in working so hard, Boaz's kind mercy and generosity, and God's kindness in providing gentle rains, good seed, fertile soil, and the divine appointment between Ruth and Boaz were finally recognized and gratefully acknowledged. All of these elements in God's story for these widows would swirl and blend to oil the hinge and open new possibilities with Naomi's next observation: "The man is a close relative of ours, one of our redeemers." (Ruth 2:20)

Instead of bitterness over all she'd lost in her past, her thoughts turned toward redemption and the future. What was going on in her mind reminds me of Romans 12:2a, "Do not be conformed to this world, but be transformed by the renewal of your mind."

Writing a blog for widows like I do requires reading blogs that widows write. It's not enough that I've been widowed; if I want to communicate effectively and connect with widows, I need to understand their current mindsets and spot their tendencies and trends. Unfortunately, what I sometimes see is a feeding frenzy of self-pity, victimization, and self-centeredness. People do get stuck in grief; it becomes their claim to fame. Afraid of more loss, there is a natural reluctance to live again, to let go of the connection with death and the spotlight of attention. The world's pattern is to consume, to feed the ego and to allow for self-absorption. It's easy to join the fray.

Grieving lends itself to a time of introspection. To a certain limit, self-centeredness is a survival skill. Yet, such a focus on self can become a trap. Allowing negative feelings to make our decisions and shape our relationships will certainly complicate and perpetuate any grief we are experiencing.

Speaking words of praise as Naomi did is one key to transforming our minds and not getting trapped in grief. We don't have to feel it to speak it. Rather, we speak from our knowledge of God, telling the facts. Praise comes from an attitude (not an emotion) of gratitude and shakes everyone into the proper slot: God is high, holy, and eternal! The universe revolves around him, not us. Realizing that, we give thanks in everything; we weep with those who weep and rejoice with those who rejoice; and we determine to trust God even when the fig tree doesn't blossom (Habakkuk 3:17-18).

In other words, we do the impossible: We trust God and praise him.

There are simple exercises to help you do this seemingly impossible task. Once you start, you'll quickly grow adept. Praise dwells inside the heart of each Christian like all the animals on Noah's ark, waiting for the flood to subside, waiting for those doors to open!

A lot of modern research makes it clear that gratitude and praise do help the soul adapt and grow through difficult times. There are suggestions and techniques for gratitude journaling, so many that the scope of this chapter cannot possibly elaborate on all of them. But perhaps an old gospel tune, published in 1897 by Johnson Oatman, Jr., summarizes it best:

> *When upon life's billows you are tempest-tossed,*
> *When you are discouraged, thinking all is lost,*
> *Count your many blessings, name them one by one,*
> *And it will surprise you what the Lord hath done.*
> *Count your blessings, name them one by one,*
> *Count your blessings, see what God hath done!*
> *Count your blessings, name them one by one,*
> *Count your many blessings, see what God hath done.*

This does not merely mean putting on a happy face or exercising the power of positive thinking. Problems don't vanish just because we whistle a happy tune and recite a few Bible verses. If you've loved, you'll grieve at the loss of that love. Counting your blessings, however, will enable you to grieve with hope, to be set free from the pattern of the world and transformed in your thinking.

Some of the Christian widows who visit my blog tell me privately, "I feel okay, but I feel guilty for feeling okay! Is there something wrong with me? Am I going to wake up some day and flip out in anger or get hit with a severe case of depression because I'm repressing or denying my grief?"

I remember secretly wondering the very same things myself. *When will I get all the anger? When will I get so depressed that I'll hole up in my house for weeks?* Sure, I cried; sure, I hollered at God; sure, I felt shock; and I certainly was sad! But I never did hit those nice, neat "stages of grief" I was waiting for.

Let me tell you that it's okay to be okay! If you've been working through your grief as best as you can, you don't have to be hounded by the fear that depression and anger are inevitable. Sure, crying spells sneak up at the most unexpected times. But then you clean up your smeared mascara and it's time to start pushing that grocery cart again.

We need not dread the so-called stages of grief. Grief is different for everyone, especially for the Christian. I Thessalonians 4:13 reminds us we do not grieve in the manner of people who have no hope. We certainly do grieve, but when we begin to practice the art of gratitude, we will begin to transform our mind and, like he did for Naomi, over time God will transform our story too.

.

*Counting your blessings is a powerful form of praise straight from the lines of Scripture. Psalm 103:2 (NIV) provides a great example as David reminds himself, "Praise the Lord, my soul, and forget not all his benefits—."*

*David then lists the many benefits offered from the Lord: forgiveness, healing, redemption, love, compassion, satisfaction, renewal, righteousness, justice, knowledge, mercy, grace, patience, longsuffering, and abundant love!*

*David puts the benefits of his relationship with God into earthly perspective throughout the rest of the psalm, describing how high and great God's love is, how far God will remove our sins from us, how this powerful God loves us like a father has compassion on his children, and that although mankind is as grass before this mighty God, his love for mankind never stops.*

*Taking these verses to heart and literally counting your blessings as David did will transform your mind and swing your own story wide open to the good plan and purpose of God.*

*Open your Bible to Psalm 103. In your notebook or journal, number the benefits God provides for you and praise him for your favorite blessings.*

Being confident of this, that he who began a good work in you will carry it on to completion until the day of Christ Jesus. (Philippians 1:6 NIV)


*Dear Lord,*

*You numbered the stars, the hairs on my head, and the grains of barley on Naomi's kitchen table. These are huge numbers, but your benefits to me are far more numerous. Like Naomi, I offer praise to you for not forgetting me and for showing me kindness and blessing.*

*Amen.*

# Chapter Fifteen

## *Taking Refuge*

And Ruth the Moabite said, "Besides, he said to me, 'You shall keep close by my young men until they have finished all my harvest.'" And Naomi said to Ruth, her daughter-in-law, "It is good, my daughter, that you go out with his young women, lest in another field you be assaulted." So she kept close to the young women of Boaz, gleaning until the end of the barley and wheat harvests. And she lived with her mother-in-law. (Ruth 2:21-23)

*Dear Orpah,*

*Here in Bethlehem they call me "the Moabite." Everywhere I go, whispers follow. I feel eyes on me. I don't look much different than anyone else, but I'm a foreigner, and some people resent me.*

*Evil lurks everywhere, even in this Promised Land. Naomi and Boaz watch out for me, though. They don't want me to be afraid, but they do want me to be careful. You should have heard Boaz order his men to leave me alone and not touch me! They sure did quit their little gestures and whistles after that!*

*I will just do what I need to do. God is watching over me too.*

*Love,*
*Ruth*

# Taking Refuge

Life isn't safe. From dangerous people like international terrorists, children with guns in schools, murderers, rapists, and robbers to natural disasters like tornadoes, earthquakes, floods or fires, danger is all around.

I wistfully sigh over memories of the peoples and lands portrayed in my childhood Sunday school classes. Flannelgraph figures of people dressed in long, colorful robes, riding donkeys or camels, growing their own grain, watching their flocks of sheep—how pastoral, peaceful, and safe that world seemed to be!

But reality interrupts my reverie. Life might have been more boring back then, but it wasn't less dangerous. Remember, Ruth's story took place during the time of the book of Judges, a messed-up and violent era, to be sure, steeped with stories of terrorists, rapists, and murderers in great abundance.

For example, in Judges 19 and 20, we find the story of a concubine who was tossed out in the street one night to appease a gang of men who wanted to have sex with her master. She was raped and abused all night long. The next morning, the girl's master found her dead body on the doorstep. He loaded her onto his donkey, and when he got home, he cut her body into twelve pieces and sent a piece to each to the twelve tribes of Israel, causing a civil war.

The Old Testament provided laws against murder, rape, theft, assault, and much more. God knows of the heinous crimes and malicious behavior that mankind is capable of, and he set vengeance and judgment in motion. It's upsetting to even think about. Maybe you're wondering, *Doesn't God protect widows? Don't widows go through enough? If God is in control, can I really prevent anything bad from happening?*

I'm not going to argue the sovereignty of God and his mysterious ways and will. Theologians and pastors have argued for centuries about these things, and none have been able to come to any sort of agreement. All I want to say is this: When we're in deep water, we need to know how to swim. Likewise, a woman needs to know a thing or two about stepping into a dangerous world. One thing theologians and pastors do agree on is that most widows are in "deep water!"

Proverbs 14:1 states, "The wisest of women builds her house…" This is a proactive statement. A wise woman doesn't neglect anything, including her safety.

Ruth was wise to take reasonable safety measures. She was, in a sense, building her house, and she submitted to advice from Boaz and Naomi. Let's look at some of the specific actions Ruth engaged to provide for her safety.

*Receive Counsel*

First, Ruth received counsel from her elders. Naomi and Boaz knew the neighborhood, so to speak. They were aware that Ruth would be misunderstood and prejudged, even though Ruth might not have realized how she, a Moabite, was being perceived. Moabites didn't have the best of reputations in Israel. They were descendants of incest between Lot and his daughters, (Genesis 19:30-38), they had tried to curse Israel during the exodus from Egypt (Numbers 22:4-6), and Moabite men were banned from the assembly of the Lord (Deuteronomy 23:3-6).

Boaz offered general advice: He told Ruth she should stay in his fields with his servant girls. Naomi gave the reason: Ruth might very well have been harmed in another field. Racism and sexual harassment were alive and well in ancient times, and they are still thriving today. Because we may be faced with these, we need to follow counsel from men and women who know God, understand the culture we're in, and will help us find a protective work environment.

*Reach Out*

Another thing Ruth did was to live with Naomi. Maybe young widows today should live with older, wiser widows; perhaps older widows should seek each other out to share housing expenses. I hope that if I'm ever widowed again I can find other widows to share a house with.

If sharing a house isn't feasible, share your life. By this, I mean you should find a wise woman to whom you can be accountable and with whom you can be transparent. Widowhood gets a little crazy at times.

It's easy to lose perspective, to start sinking in those treacherous depths. A trusted, wise friend can reinforce our decisions or help us know if, when, and how to correct our actions.

## Be Aware of Vulnerabilities

Let's face it, when we're grieving, we are vulnerable.

"We know of a woman whose husband died just like yours did," a visiting missionary couple told me after church one Sunday. "The death was sudden, unexpected. She never got a chance to say 'goodbye' either. Everyone thought she was doing okay. She kept working full time as a hair stylist. She had some life insurance money and was taking time to think and sort through her options. Last we heard, though, a man had come into her small town and gotten a job at the same salon where she worked. He gave her some special attention, and she fell in love. She got swindled. All her money is gone now, and so is he."

According to Judith Nichols Moore, President of Widows International, an organization that has faithfully served widows in the name of the Lord for many years, there are people out there who purposely read the obituaries with the intent of finding unsuspecting widows whom they can take advantage of.[1]

Widows are vulnerable. Emotions are raw and the mind is numb. Some are so exhausted by the stress and change that they are incapable of saying "No!" to anything. Moore went on to say that she's seen family members drain a widow's finances or withhold food or visits with the grandchildren. They might even abuse the poor woman emotionally, threatening to lock her away in a nursing home or government housing.[2] I'm not saying this to incite fear. I merely hope to alert you. I want to assure you that when a red flag pops up in your mind, you need to pay attention to it and seek protection.

## Be Accountable

Miriam Neff, in her book *From One Widow to Another*, suggests that a widow gather around her a "board of directors" as soon as possible. This isn't as complicated as it sounds; it's a tangible model for finding your own Naomi and Boaz, people you need in your life. Neff suggests that you seek out six dependable people, but the model is flexible. You may find more, or you might find some people who fill two of the roles mentioned below:[3]

1. A godly widow

2. A person with financial wisdom

3. A practical friend

4. An encourager

5. Someone with spiritual discernment and courage

6. A relative whose priority is your wellbeing

An assortment of people like this will be used of God to help you make wise decisions. Now is not the time to depend on family members who are also grieving and working through their own issues.

Instead, take advantage of the benefits of being a part of God's family. Let the body of Christ serve you in this capacity, but do not sit back and expect your pastor or women's Bible study leader to volunteer for these positions or assign people to help you. You must ask. Let me say that again: *YOU must ask!*

Most people simply have no knowledge of what a widow needs. Before you became one, had you ever anticipated the needs of widows or prepared for the experience yourself? You likely hadn't, and neither have your friends. Nevertheless, that doesn't mean they aren't equipped to help you. No one will know whether or not they can help you until you ask them and explain what sort of help you need. I encourage you to read the details of the board member positions and their job descriptions in Miriam's book for valuable insights.

In this land of widowhood, this land of grief, a place where we are foreigners, we need to understand that not everyone views widows with sympathy and benevolence. Just as Ruth dealt with stigma as a Moabite, being a widow today may signal exploitation and opportunity to evil people.

This doesn't mean we need to be so afraid that we lock our doors and never come out; it only means we need to be careful. We need to know our surroundings. In addition, we need to find a Naomi or Boaz of our own, someone who knows the neighborhood. A Naomi is an experienced widow who can guide us through the roller coaster ride of grief. A Boaz might be any man or woman who can provide practical help with their network of business contacts and personal resources.

There's also the larger community and government. We are privileged to live in a country that has, for the most part, an approachable and responsive government and judicial system. If you run into problems with government agencies, banks, or Social Security, contact your state senator and representatives. Their contact information is available on the editorial page of daily local newspapers, the Internet, your phone book, and elsewhere. In your neighborhood, you can speak with the local police department and let them know your situation and address. In smaller communities, they might even note your property and will keep a close watch on your house when they do their rounds in the first few weeks, especially while you're away at calling hours or during the funeral or memorial services.

Find out ways to protect yourself from identity theft and be careful when answering the telephone (or the door) and giving out information. It's very upsetting when telemarketers ask to speak to your husband. Tell them, "He can't come to the phone right now." Do NOT tell them he's dead, because that might be the information they're looking for. My friend Eva had her house broken into after such an instance and a series of hang-up phone calls. Don't hesitate to look into a security plan if you are worried about unusual callers.

One day when I came home, I noticed the front door of my house hanging wide open and the storm door unlatched, swinging back and forth with the breeze! I didn't have a cell phone with me, so I simply backed right out of the driveway and went over to a neighbor's house. Given the situation—it was broad daylight, my house was highly visible, and it was most likely that my teenage children had already come and gone from school without latching the door—my neighbor simply came and walked through the house with me. He looked for bogeymen and made sure nothing had been vandalized or stolen. If someone had been in the house, it would have been better to have the police with me, but at least I didn't have to go in and check it out myself. That would have been foolish.

Some dangers, like unexpected earthquakes and tornados, can't be avoided. Others, like walking alone at night, leaving your doors unlocked, and being gullible and vulnerable, are like going out in deep water when you don't know how to swim.

In order to navigate grief, take refuge in the circle of safe people God has provided. When you do, you'll be better able to work through the daily challenges and pressures of widowhood.

*Answering these questions will help you identify some of your personal safety issues and help you consider a mentoring or house-sharing relationship with other widows.*

*What good, valuable, trustworthy advice have I heard from the people in my life?*

*What is the first thing I need to do to follow this advice?*

*What scares me the most?*

*Who are three other women I can talk with about this fear?*

*If the opportunity arose, would I want to share living expenses with another widow or widows?*

*What would be some of the advantages? The disadvantages?*

*Is there a particular situation, some deep water, that I'm in right now that makes me uncomfortable?*

*God has appointed governments and laws to protect people. What sort of authorities (state and local government agencies, church authorities, laws, etc.) can I go to for help? List names or offices and phone numbers below:*

Police: _____

Lawyer: _____

Pastor: _____

Hospital: _____

Fire Department: _____

Other: _____

Save me, O God, for the waters have come up to my neck. (Psalm 69:1)

*Dear Lord,*

*Please protect me from danger and help me not be overly fearful. Keep me alert, help me listen to advice as if it's straight from you, and open my eyes to other women who would be good mentors or housemates for me.*

*Amen.*

# Section Four
# Waiting

# Chapter Sixteen

## *Facing the Future*

Then Naomi her mother-in-law said to her, "My daughter, should I not seek rest for you, that it may be well with you? Is not Boaz our relative, with whose young women you were? See, he is winnowing barley tonight at the threshing floor. Wash therefore and anoint yourself, and put on your cloak and go down to the threshing floor, but do not make yourself known to the man until he has finished eating and drinking. But when he lies down, observe the place where he lies. Then go and uncover his feet and lie down, and he will tell you what to do." And she replied, "All that you say I will do." (Ruth 3:1-5)

*Dear Orpah,*

*It's been several weeks since we arrived in Bethlehem. Every day is the same: I go out and glean with Boaz's maidservants, and Naomi studies law. She's found two separate Hebrew laws that could help us: kinsman-redeemer (Leviticus 25:25), and levirate marriage (Deuteronomy 25:5-6). Levirate marriage would provide us with husbands, but the kinsman-redeemer law would also get her land back. She's been waiting for her relatives to act on either one, but there's no word.*

*I think they've forgotten about us, but Naomi thinks that the two of us, being two widows from one family, present a unique legal situation. The next of kin just don't know what to do with us.*

*She's watching for the perfect opportunity. "God will provide," she says.*

*"Nothing will separate us," is what I say.*

*Love,*
*Ruth*

# Facing the Future

Naomi and Ruth survived the journey through the Judean wilderness. They found a place to stay in Bethlehem, Ruth found favor at her job, and Naomi was blessed by the kindness of Boaz, yet both still faced a lifetime of loneliness ahead. They had each other, but their friendship didn't drive away the oppressing quiet that clung to the walls of their house nor the nagging problems of singleness and an unsecured future.

They had worries to consider: What would happen to Ruth if Naomi died? What would happen to Naomi if Ruth died? It wasn't a good prospect for either, but it seemed Naomi was intent on facing it and finding a solution. Scripture doesn't say she studied the laws of Israel as Ruth refers to in our postcard storyline, but Naomi knew how the laws worked. She'd discovered that in addition to gleaning, God had set up other ways to provide for widows. Why else would she have told her widowed daughter-in-law to propose to Boaz?

Do you recall how Naomi prayed that Ruth and Orpah would receive kindness and find rest in Ruth 1? Naomi did, and she was still waiting for God to fully answer that prayer! Even though she'd been angry with God, she had still believed in God, and she believed he answered prayer. Now, weeks later, she waited expectantly. She also understood that God might use her actions and obedience to answer her own prayer.[1] As Ruth gleaned the barley harvest, Naomi watched for a harvest of answered prayer.

*Naomi Wasn't Passive*

When God answers prayer, it's always according to his will, and that's always within the framework of his law and character. That's why we go to church and Bible studies, so we can understand God and his ways and recognize how he works in our lives and how he'd have us behave and implement his ways.

With similar intent, Naomi must have learned about God's law and character. She found out about two Old Testament laws that would answer her prayer and help Ruth's future. The kinsman-redeemer law spelled out that a relative should help a poverty-stricken family recover their land. The levirate marriage law allowed a widow to marry her deceased husband's relative so she could have a son with him, thus carrying on the family name and property. Both these laws could be enforced or activated to help in Naomi's case. As Naomi waited and watched, it became evident to her that she was the one God would use to initiate these laws.

When she had asked God to meet the core needs of her daughters-in-law—kindness and rest—the measurable, visible plumb line for recognizing God's answer was that they'd find rest in the home of another husband. (Ruth 1:9) In that day and age, Naomi knew Ruth needed a husband, and she saw Boaz as a perfect match. Anyone can come up with a plan, but it always takes a certain risk—at times called "faith"—to put the plan into action.

## She Waited

Weeks followed. The barley harvest, which always ran from the end of April through May, had ended. The wheat harvest began, so we can safely assume it was June. It had been almost two months since their return to Bethlehem, and Naomi's prayer hadn't yet been answered. Was it a constant "pray without ceasing" sort of passion for Naomi? From the extraordinary courage we're about to see, I believe so. James 5:16 says "The prayer of a righteous person has great power as it is working." Naomi and Ruth stood at the ready for a powerful, effective answer to prayer.

Naomi wisely watched, waited, and planned. She was not impatient or impetuous, and she gave herself time to form a thoughtful, detailed, and precisely targeted plan. Most importantly, her plan left the entire outcome to God. She didn't hover or fret about it, but she did think ahead, and she was prepared to act when God orchestrated the circumstances we'll see in the next chapter.

## Naomi Loved

It's crucial to realize that Naomi put Ruth's interests ahead of her own. Most people think of Naomi as an elderly, feeble woman without very many of her own years left, but I'm not so sure about that. Consider how strong and healthy she must have been to have walked fifty or more miles from Moab to Bethlehem. Also, when I look ahead to Ruth 4:15, the women speak of a good future for Naomi, one in which she is renewed and happy. It seemed the people of the village thought there was still a life ahead for Naomi. How would that have been possible if Naomi was so feeble? Perhaps her statement, "I'm too old to have a husband," at the beginning of her journey was just an outburst of dismay. Perhaps Naomi should have been the bride instead of Ruth. In all my research, no one has ever asked that question, but maybe it should be considered. Sure, she could have been seventy or more years old, but it's more likely, in my opinion, that she was in her forties or early fifties.

In any case, we see that Naomi's plan refused to vie over a husband and secure a future of her own. Everything she initiated was to protect Ruth's best interests. Naomi modeled New Testament living even though she existed during Old Testament times. She did exactly what Romans 12:10 (NIV) commands us to do: "Be devoted to one another in love. Honor one another above yourselves."

I have a feeling Naomi could have married Boaz; after all, she had "first rights." Perhaps she simply did not want to remarry. I find some widows today like Naomi. It's not that they can't remarry; they just don't want to. They see themselves as God's individual creation. They are content with their personal identity and accepting of their lot, even preferring it to remarriage. Compare this to the majority of widowers who can't seem to function without a wife. I recall that when God created Adam, he created Eve to help him, but he didn't create anyone to help Eve! Women were designed by God to be helpmates, not to necessarily need a helpmate. I think we women are far better equipped to handle solo living than men are.

Ruth, on the other hand, seemed interested in Boaz. At her initial contact with Boaz when she said, "You have comforted me and spoken kindly to your servant," (Ruth 2:13) we catch the slightest hint of how much Boaz might have meant to her. That was the only romance up to that point in the story. But now Naomi would encourage Ruth to propose to the man! Naomi basically told her, "Dress up like a bride and go ask him to marry you."

That's what I call faith. As I imagine myself in Naomi's sandals and then in Ruth's, I realize that when I pray—and pray for something specific—God might open up doors of opportunity and love that will require huge risk, courage, and a closer walk with him than could have ever been imagined. As such, I can face the future. He might even use me as an instrument to answer my own prayers!

*I hope you've been praying for kindness and rest for a while now as you've been reading this book. Have you seen any answers yet? If so, jot them down here on this page or in your notebook. Details aren't necessary. Just write enough to jog your memory in the future.*

*Is God asking you to do anything more than pray for these situations or opportunities? Remember that Naomi's actions were in accordance with God's Word, so she's a good example to follow. God may also lead you through counsel from wise and godly people in your life.*

*If you haven't prayed for kindness and rest for yourself, take some time to consider why not. Is it simply procrastination or disinterest, or is there a deeper reluctance?*

*Regarding remarriage, check the response that best describes your current wish:*

___Never. Remarriage is not for me. I have absolutely no desire for that.

___Probably not. I think it's a statistical impossibility.

___Maybe, if I meet the right man.

___I'll do anything to get married again.

___I'm not ready to risk losing another husband.

Let the morning bring me word of your unfailing love, for I have put my trust in you. Show me the way I should go, for to you I entrust my life. (Psalm 143:8)

*Dear God,*

*Please give me courage to carry through with my prayers and see any answers or opportunities you provide. Thank you that whether or not I marry again, I can be assured that your love will never fail. I trust you to show me the way I should go, and I'm putting my future in your hands.*

*Amen.*

# Chapter Seventeen

## *Protecting Virtue*

So she went down to the threshing floor and did just as her mother-in-law had commanded her. And when Boaz had eaten and drunk, and his heart was merry, he went to lie down at the end of the heap of grain. Then she came softly and uncovered his feet and lay down. (Ruth 3:6-7)

*Dear Orpah,*

*Do you remember the story we heard as children, the one about how the Moabite women in the north seduced the men of Israel with the sexual rituals of Baal worship? (Numbers 25:1-2) All Moabite girls wanted to grow up to be like them! They almost destroyed Israel! Our men were great at war, but our women were great at seduction. Israel, too, remembers this story. I know because of the names and remarks some of the men make when I pass by. They know we were raised with very different morals.*

*Boaz and I will be together tonight, a man and a woman. Naomi sees that we are attracted to each other, but amazingly, this has nothing to do with seduction. This is something different, something so much better!*

*Love,*
*Ruth*

# Protecting Virtue

Let's face it: At some point, you'll probably think of dating again. Maybe you've reached that point already. But what will happen if you do? Television shows, movies, magazine articles, and books want you to believe that casual sex between consenting adults is acceptable—even sensible if you're thinking about marrying the person, something like test-driving a car. This is the bed-hopping philosophy our pop culture pushes. These days, teenagers are either aware of or actually participating in "sexting"—text messaging nude photos or dirty messages; some of them have more sexual experience than many adults. Virgins are oddities and even scorned and mocked. And, the world tells us, certainly a grown woman, sexually mature and experienced, has needs and urges and the right to see them satisfied, right? Are you ready to step into this world of moral dilemma and sexual compromise?

Naomi, Ruth, and Boaz show us ways to avoid sexual temptation. They are fine examples of a higher calling: protecting virtue.

When we choose to look out for the other person, to love and respect them so much that protecting their virtue and reputation is more important than fulfilling our own needs and lusts, we can avoid sexual sin.

## Make Personal Righteousness a Priority

At the top of the list for these Bible characters was God's law. The Ten Commandments in Exodus 20 were foundational in their thinking, and though they were written by God's own finger ages ago, these commands offer us a concise guide to morality today.

Consider the following: "You shall have no other gods before me." (Exodus 20:3) Sometimes the line between what we love or think we need and what we worship becomes very muddled. We need to be sure that in dating or in our desire to find a husband, we don't expect a man to fulfill spiritual needs and heal the heartache that only God can satisfy. Unconditional love, forgiveness, security, loneliness, contentment, and peace cannot be perfectly provided by another human being. Ever. Even our dearly departed husband did not always perfectly meet all needs.

Don't be afraid of needs or the anxious feelings they stir. The needs we yearn for help us recognize desires and emotions we can be honest about with God. Tell God what you need and let *him* decide how your needs will be supplied. God has promised to take care of us; therefore, our needs are his problems.

Exodus 20:14 commands, "You shall not commit adultery." God says this more plainly than I dare: Don't have sex outside of marriage. There—plain and simple. Also, it's for our own good. Think of all the broken hearts—broken wives, husbands, and children who could have been spared the destruction of adultery. God didn't give us this commandment to make us miserable. He gave it because he loves us and doesn't want us or our loved ones to suffer the consequences of foolish, self-serving actions!

The list of commandments goes on. Exodus 20:17 adds, "You shall not covet…" God doesn't want us to envy or desire things that belong to another, including husbands! It doesn't matter if a man tells you he doesn't love his wife anymore. If he's married, don't even let your mind utter a wishful little sigh when he walks by. That's coveting! Sometimes daydreams and self-pity lead to covetousness; we need to guard our thoughts and control our impulses.

Keeping a clear conscience before God in the areas of idolatry, adultery, and covetousness provide a strong moral backbone for righteous dating behavior.

*Respect Your Date's Public Reputation*

Boaz was "a man of standing," well known and honored in Bethlehem. The picture of Ruth at his feet in the middle of the night at the threshing floor sounds peculiar to us, but I believe Naomi timed their rendezvous to protect Boaz.

Under Old Testament law and social custom, it was perfectly acceptable for a widow to ask a man to marry her. The problem for the man was that if he refused her proposal, it would be seen as a *faux pas*, a social smudge on his character. (Deuteronomy 25:7-9). Maybe Naomi realized that the only time in Boaz's schedule when he and Ruth could be perfectly alone was that night on the threshing floor. Ruth could pop the question there, in private, and Boaz wouldn't be publicly humiliated if he declined.

So Naomi instructed Ruth to do it all quietly, then to wait for Boaz's instructions. She quite literally put their lives in his hands. He could have demanded that Ruth go home and never speak to him again. He could have destroyed their hope for a marriage and kinsman-redeemer with one little word: "No."

I believe there was an unspoken agreement between Naomi and Ruth that they would not gossip, manipulate, or backstab if they didn't like Boaz's reply. They were women of honor. The man's good name in the community was more important to them than their own welfare, emotions, or desire to be connected to him. They loved him enough to respect his reputation.

### Love Your Date Enough to Protect His Personal Virtue

And love yourself and your children enough to protect your own! Protection is a higher love, transcending passion and sex. Boaz and Ruth knew what sexual tension was. Put yourself in their place: two mature adults, interested in each other, together in the privacy of darkness. *Hmm.* Isn't that the stuff of those paperback romance novels?

In fact, the whole scene of uncovering Boaz's feet and spending the night together is fraught with innuendo. The word for "feet" in Hebrew[1] could mean everything below a man's waistline, and we can easily guess what would happen then! But still, the only thing that happened was a conversation of sweetness, vulnerability, and mutual respect.

It was not a sexual encounter. Adultery was punishable by death; Ruth could have been stoned rather than given a place in history. That night, an honorable man and an honorable woman chose personal righteousness over easy sex.

### Don't Settle for Just Anyone

As you read ahead a few verses in the story, Boaz exclaimed that Ruth could have chosen younger men, either rich or poor. She could have had her pick of the men in Bethlehem! She was the sort of woman who would have made a great wife for any man, but she was astute enough to know that not just any man would be a great husband for her. Perhaps in her first marriage, she'd learned that love is animated; it grows and deepens when rooted in good character and advised by wise people such as Naomi. Ruth realized that youth, sex, wealth, and ambition are fragile attractions. Boaz, probably closer in age to Naomi, was far better than the younger men. We'll soon see that while she respected his reputation and protected his virtue, Boaz proved exemplary protection and respect for her.

My curiosity grew as I saw that Ruth entered her second marriage engagement with thoughtfulness and honor far outweighing today's standard of attraction and romance.

Her actions, carried out under the cover of that night, proved to be logical and rational for the context of her ancient culture. This intriguing scene lived out by Ruth nourished my soul and opened my mind up to wonder, *Would loving someone again be as different, as new, and as full of butterflies as it was the first time?* Just being able to ask that question was a huge step closer to home on the widows' path.

*It's never too early in widowhood to consider motives and set some safeguards into your lifestyle that will encourage personal righteousness and protect virtue in dating. Examine your heart motive for dating. Pray honestly to God about it. Remember that looking to a person to meet spiritual needs that only God can meet is like idolatry.*

*Consider safe ways to meet good men. Will you depend on mutual friends and co-workers, church groups, or community groups for introductions? Will you try Internet single sites, social networking, or chat rooms? Will job travels or vacations introduce you to men?*

*Enforce these boundaries:*

- Remain relatively anonymous on the Internet. Don't post your phone number, address, full name, or even the specific city you live in.

- Enjoy the security of group dates when you are just getting to know someone.

- Always let someone know when you have a date. Give them details of time, place, and activity. Accountability is good for your conscience and your safety.

- Avoid overnight situations.

- Respect your friends' and family's opinions about your date. They can see things you can't.

Search me, O God, and know my heart! Try me and know my thoughts! And see if there be any grievous way in me, and lead me in the way everlasting! (Psalm 139:23-24)

*Dear God,*

*I don't want to hide anything from you, but there are only so many cold showers I can take! Show me how to be righteous, loving, and pleasing to you and to keep your commandments as my highest authority. At the same time, open me up to love and wonder.*

*Amen.*

# Chapter Eighteen

*Trusting God in the Dark*

At midnight the man was startled and turned over, and behold, a woman lay at his feet! He said, "Who are you?" And she answered, "I am Ruth, your servant. Spread your wings over your servant, for you are a redeemer." And he said, "May you be blessed by the Lord, my daughter. You have made this last kindness greater than the first in that you have not gone after young men, whether poor or rich. And now, my daughter, do not fear. I will do for you all that you ask, for all my fellow townsmen know that you are a worthy woman. And now it is true that I am a redeemer. Yet there is a redeemer nearer than I. Remain tonight, and in the morning, if he will redeem you, good; let him do it. But if he is not willing to redeem you, then, as the Lord lives, I will redeem you. Lie down until the morning." (Ruth 3:8-13)

*Dear Orpah,*

*Ruth is on her way to the threshing floor right now. She looks beautiful, and her perfume is divine — not too heavy, but just enough to carry a hint in the evening air.*

*Meanwhile, I'm a nervous wreck! What if anyone sees her? They'll think she's a prostitute! What if she can't find Boaz? Or worse, what if she takes a wrong turn in the dark and lies at the feet of someone else? You know, the men sleep there to guard the harvest from raiders. What if there really is an attack tonight and I've put Ruth in the middle of it?*

*I don't think I'll sleep a wink.*

*Love,*

*Naomi*

# Trusting God in the Dark

Can you imagine if Naomi had written out her schedule and scheme in a planner or calendar like we do today?

*Naomi's Planner*

Her to-do list before the move back to Bethlehem might have looked something like this:

✓ *Sell everything.*

✓ *Pack water bottles, a change of clothes, dried fruits, nuts, unleavened bread, a mantle for sleeping at night.*

✓ *Find a shepherd's staff to use as a walking stick and weapon.*

Her calendar would have had these days circled in red marker, along with memos in big block lettering and the following plans noted:

✓ *Mid-April — LEAVE FOR BETHLEHEM*

✓ *Four Days Later — ARRIVE IN BETHLEHEM, FIND HOUSING*

✓ *End of April — BARLEY HARVEST BEGINS (Ruth — will look for a job as a gleaner. Naomi — will study property and inheritance laws, widows rights, and what to do when there are two widows and only one piece of property.)*

✔ *End of May — WHEAT HARVEST BEGINS, BARLEY GETS THRESHED (Naomi — find a good husband for Ruth and make sure there are no other eligible parties or loopholes! Ruth — ask him to marry her! )*

Her planner for the evening described in Ruth 3 might have had these scribbles:

✔ *Help Ruth bathe.*

✔ *Borrow that amazing perfume from the neighbor, but don't arouse her suspicions!*

✔ *Clean the shawl so Ruth can sleep in it or wrap up in it if she gets chilly.*

✔ *Make sure Boaz is still going to the threshing floor.*

Naomi was too busy to notice that the villagers in Bethlehem never called her the bitter name "Mara," as she'd demanded when she'd first returned. Had she finally recovered from her grief? Does anyone ever really recover from grief, as if it is some kind of sickness that we can forget about once the fever is over? Only Naomi knew the answers to those personal questions, but what we see from her actions is that she was moving on, involved in life, and anticipating the future. That was a healthy and hopeful reaction to a painful and desperate situation.

The process of planning and looking forward to an event in the future is therapeutic, even if it's not as monumental as a marriage proposal. When widows ask me for a quick piece of advice, I tell them, "Give yourself something to look forward to. It can be a visit, a vacation, or something as small as a free concert in the city park or a Sunday afternoon drive. Be your own best friend. Make a date with yourself for whatever makes you smile."

I picture Naomi smiling. Her planning helped her focus on redemption and filled her heart with hope.

*Ruth's Plan*

Ruth also had a plan. She agreed to do everything Naomi told her to do, but unknown to Naomi, she devised a plan that went beyond Naomi's instructions. Compare Naomi's orders to Ruth with what Ruth actually did: Naomi told her to find out where Boaz lay, uncover his feet, and then lay down. She said, "He will tell you what to do." (Ruth 3:4) Naomi didn't instruct Ruth to say anything to Boaz. But look at what Ruth did! She asked Boaz to spread his "wings" over her since he was a kinsman-redeemer. Spreading his wings implied a home for Naomi too. You see, Naomi's selfless instructions would have only secured a future for Ruth. There was nothing in it for Naomi.[1]

The most beautiful thing of all was that both widows focused their plans on helping the other more than looking out for themselves. Naomi's plan was to take care of Ruth, but Ruth's plan was to take care of Naomi.

*Boaz's Plan*

Boaz was surprised by Ruth's visit and request, but his quick evaluation of it presented a problem; he didn't realize Naomi had already figured out he was the only eligible or interested kinsman! He only knew there was another kinsman-redeemer ahead of him in line. Boaz immediately planned to go to town the next morning and take care of the legal end of the proposal.

Doesn't it sound like they were already a family? Isn't that the way families work in the real world? Oh, it'd be ideal if the parents or "head of the household" made all the plans, but in reality, each person has their own. In a good setting, these plans unselfishly contribute to the benefit of the whole and bring about harmony. Each family member adjusts his or her ideas to the bigger agenda.

*God's Plan*

God's plan kicked into this story in a very subtle way. There was one small detail Naomi and Ruth hadn't considered: What if Boaz hadn't awoken until it was light and Ruth would have had to leave before she had a chance to propose? Naomi, Ruth, and Boaz each played a part in the larger plan of Ruth proposing to Boaz. They fit together like puzzle pieces, but it was God who insured that his will was accomplished.

Naomi's potential worries (*What if Ruth can't find Boaz? What if Boaz doesn't want to marry Ruth?*) were true possibilities. But once again, Naomi stepped out in faith. She had made her plans, detailed and thorough. She was a smart lady and used the brain God had given her. Still, though, the smartest thing she did was to let go and leave it in God's hands. She didn't tag along with Ruth to satisfy her own curiosity or make sure everything went just right. Naomi did what she could, and when events moved out of her hands, she let them.

How long do you think Ruth waited at the feet of Boaz before he woke up? Five minutes? Ten? Two hours? Longer? Think of how alone Ruth might have felt, waiting and wondering in the dark. How often have we widows felt the very same way? At least figuratively speaking, we are in the dark too. Sometimes we're powerless to affect our circumstances. All we can do is wait for someone to wake up and help us.

Yet God sees us just as he saw Ruth patiently waiting under the stars with the smell of threshed barley cooling in the night air. God designs these waiting times for us, when all we can hear is the nothingness of his silence. Our hearts yearn and strain for him to show himself, but dark times are not for seeing; rather, they are for listening. Life might appear motionless and blank in those moments, but there is a current underneath, and the waiting makes us stronger. Waiting is the isometric exercise of the soul and our faith.

Then, like a conductor interpreting a symphony, God plays out each moment of our day to a length of his choice while we wait. Some of those moments are brisk eighth notes, some are steady quarter notes, and others sound the heavy whole notes, holding entire measures with one lonely groan. And then, when we least expect it, he moves, like a conductor raising his baton. Did you notice at the very beginning of this scene? Look at Ruth 3:8: "At midnight the man was startled …"

I believe God chose that moment in the story to let us know he was still in control. Naomi, Ruth and Boaz had actively planned, but God was the only one with any real control. Ruth didn't reach over and poke old Boaz, Boaz didn't wake himself up or set an alarm clock, and Naomi didn't send an extra player upon the scene. No, Boaz was startled with a wakeup call that came from God.

Boaz might have missed the opportunity and slept soundly all night. Ruth could have made a terrible mistake and lain at the feet of another man. But Boaz was startled. Why? How? Because God was on the scene! All our plans depend on God's attention and direction to the details we can't control.

Naomi, Ruth, and Boaz each had a plan, just as you and I make plans. For them and for us, though, God's plan overrules all others.

Can we accept that? Like Ruth, can we follow godly instructions? Can we set our own plans but trust God for the outcome?

Trusting God in the dark can be terrifying. But understanding that God plans, too, and that his plans pick up the details we cannot possibly control is a startling trail marker on the widows' path.

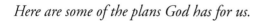

*Here are some of the plans God has for us.*

*Place a checkmark by any that speak to you today.*

❑ Many, Lord my God, are the wonders you have done, the things you planned for us. (Psalm 40:5 NIV)

❑ Let the one who walks in the dark, who has no light, trust in the name of the Lord and rely on their God. (Isaiah 50:10b NIV)

❑ For I know the plans I have for you," declares the Lord, "plans to prosper you and not to harm you, plans to give you hope and a future. (Jeremiah 29:11 NIV)

❑ For we are God's handiwork, created in Christ Jesus to do good works, which God prepared in advance for us to do. (Ephesians 2:10 NIV)

❑ And the God of all grace, who called you to his eternal glory in Christ, after you have suffered a little while, will himself restore you and make you strong, firm and steadfast. (I Peter 5:10 NIV)

❑ Rejoice always, pray continually, give thanks in all circumstances; for this is God's will for you in Christ Jesus. (I Thessalonians 5:16-18 NIV)

Many are the plans in a person's heart, but it is the Lord's purpose that prevails. (Proverbs 19:21 NIV)

*Dear Lord,*

*I'm not sure I want to accept your plan. So far, it's broken my heart and put me in a hard place. My heart is beating as hard as Ruth's must have been when she was waiting in the dark at the feet of Boaz. By faith I will make my plans, but in faith I pray that your plan prevails. Startle me with your comfort.*

*Amen.*

# Chapter Nineteen

### *Recognizing Your Boaz*

A nd he said, "May you be blessed by the Lord, my daughter. You have made this last kindness greater than the first in that you have not gone after young men, whether poor or rich. And now, my daughter, do not fear. I will do for you all that you ask, for all my fellow townsmen know that you are a worthy woman. And now it is true that I am a redeemer. Yet there is a redeemer nearer than I. Remain tonight, and in the morning, if he will redeem you, good; let him do it. But if he is not willing to redeem you, then, as the Lord lives, I will redeem you. Lie down until the morning."

So she lay at his feet until the morning, but arose before one could recognize another. And he said, "Let it not be known that the woman came to the threshing floor." And he said, "Bring the garment you are wearing and hold it out." So she held it, and he measured out six measures of barley and put it on her. Then she went into the city. And when she came to her mother-in-law, she said, "How did you fare, my daughter?" Then she told her all that the man had done for her, saying, "These six measures of barley he gave to me, for he said to me, 'You must not go back empty-handed to your mother-in-law.'" She replied, "Wait, my daughter, until you learn how the matter turns out, for the man will not rest but will settle the matter today." (Ruth 3:10-18)

*Dear Orpah,*

*I'm thinking of a new home-based business: matchmaking! Wouldn't I be a natural at it?*

*Ruthie was my first client. I sent her to propose to Boaz last night. It's a long story with all sorts of legal maneuverings having to do with my land and the fact that Boaz was afraid I wanted to marry him. Hah!*

*Anyway, now we have to wait...but it won't be long.*

*Much love,*
*Naomi*

*PS. Ruth is in love! It was love at first sight for both of them.*

# Recognizing Your Boaz

The weirdest week of my life was the Monday after Thanksgiving, when Tom and I shared our first phone call. We had met online on a Christian singles site and had emailed back and forth for a few months. We had planned the call in advance to celebrate my surviving a dreaded oral exam—not with a dentist, but with a sadistic professor in a graduate class earlier that day! The rest of the class and I were tortured and toyed with one-by-one with as he postulated a question and called on one of his victims to answer it out loud in front of everyone, no pencils or papers allowed!

I'd survived the exam, but I didn't know if I'd survive the phone call! I'd never heard Tom's voice before. I worried, *What if he sounds goofy, like SpongeBob SquarePants or all aggressive like Rush Limbaugh? Or what if he's the "strong and silent" type?* (I can't tolerate much dead air time on the phone. I start babbling—nervously.) *Or worse yet, what if his voice is kind of husky and drop-dead sexy?* Eek!

The phone rang. I answered, and it was him! Come on girlfriends, scream for me!

His voice was normal, thank goodness. I relaxed; it was merely a phone call from a friend. There I was, sitting at the table in my little kitchen near Cleveland, and there was a man—a real, live man!—on the other end of the phone up in the Adirondack Mountains.

*But wait…what did he just say? He's in a suburb of Cleveland? A business trip? And he wants to take me out to dinner tomorrow? Eek again!*

And that was where things got weird. First, instead of feeling like I was being stalked, I started laughing. I thought it was a great joke. Weirder still—I couldn't go out to dinner because the next day I had a date! (*Two dates in one week?* I'd hardly had one date in two years). It was embarrassing to tell him I had a previous engagement. But since I would be free on Wednesday, we scheduled our first date for then.

By February, things were serious between us. February is a whammy of a month for me. Valentine's Day is fraught with memories, both good and downright awful. February 15 is the anniversary of Bruce's death, and February 16 is my birthday. I'd often wished for a fast forward button on my life when February came around, but it was on February 17 that Tom proposed to me. Of course I gave him a resounding, "YES!" After all, he was my Boaz.

If you fall in love with a man like Boaz, you will be a fortunate and beloved woman.

We've already seen many good qualities in Boaz. He was a good employer, cheerful, caring, and respected in the community.

When he and Ruth were on the brink of a marriage contract, we saw him up close and personal with Ruth. He exemplified all the qualities of a good husband in the way he treated her.

## Boaz Put God First

"May you be blessed by the Lord, my daughter," he said. As soon as he discovered Ruth was the woman at his feet, he revealed his godly compassion for her. A woman can spend a lifetime with a man whose first words are a blessing to her.

## Boaz Appreciated and Understood Ruth's Actions and Character

The act of Ruth lying at his feet was the marriage proposal; she didn't have to say a word. But when she added that he was a kinsman-redeemer as we saw in the last chapter, she essentially wrote a clause into the proposal that included Naomi, indicating it was a package deal.[1] Boaz immediately recognized this and admired her for her unselfish kindness.

## Boaz Was Sensitive to Her Potential Fear

"Don't be afraid," he said. Even if she hadn't been afraid, those were still good words to hear. They indicated that Boaz was a sensitive man with a natural instinct to protect and reassure the people he loved.

## Boaz Didn't Make a Promise He Wasn't Sure He Could Keep

At that point, Boaz wasn't positive that Ruth had the right man. He was more than willing to marry her, but if another relative had the legal prerogative, Boaz would sacrifice his own interests in order to honor the law.

These are admirable qualities to look for in a man still today: unquestionable character, above reproach, and law-abiding.

*Boaz Was Concerned for Her Safety and Reputation*

It was safer for Ruth to stay with him than for her to go home in the dark. At dawn, he sent her off in secret so no one would see her and question her virtue and reputation.

*Boaz Was Generous and Well Mannered*

Sending Ruth home loaded with grain was a gentleman's pledge to Naomi that he would provide for them both. It was respectful to Naomi and pictured that in him, she would also find redemption. Naomi, who had left Bethlehem with her husband and sons so many years earlier, only to return empty and destitute, found herself suddenly on the verge of receiving more abundance than she could hold.

*Boaz Accepted Ruth's Strength*

The grain Boaz gave Ruth weighed fifty-eight to ninety-five pounds![2] This might not have meant anything in that day–maybe all the women carried such heavy loads–but it shows me the confidence Boaz had in Ruth. He was comfortable around a strong woman.

*Boaz Didn't Procrastinate.*

Naomi, an excellent judge of character, said it best: "The man will not rest." Boaz was efficient and business-like when it came to keeping his promise. He was sensitive to the precarious situation of Ruth and Naomi. Perhaps he regretted that they'd been left to suffer in limbo for so many weeks while everyone overlooked their case and did nothing.

*Boaz Was Financially Secure*

Boaz was godly, smart, sensitive, honorable, generous, polite, accepting, and efficient. What more could a bride ask for? Oh, and he had more money than Ruth too. Money may become a crucial issue among other family members when considering remarriage. Make your decisions with the help of a wise financial counselor. Both bride and groom should have their estates in legal order. Draw up your wills, and you may even want to consider a pre-nuptial agreement if either of you have future adoption matters, or trusts, adult children, guardianships, etc.

## The Naomi Factor

It was nice that God put Ruth and Boaz together, as well as Tom and me, but how would these experiences apply to anyone else? The point I want to make is that Ruth couldn't have found Boaz without Naomi, and I couldn't have found Tom without my girlfriend Laura.

I met Laura about two months before Bruce died. She and her husband were married by Bruce and had started attending our church. We'd gone out to dinner with them once, and that was about all I knew of her. Still, after Bruce died, Laura was one of the few people brave enough to enter my life. I understood why after a few visits: She was well acquainted with death. Laura lived with cystic fibrosis.

For Laura, the hospital was a home away from home. She was there for three or four treatments a year, each lasting weeks at a time. The cystic fibrosis patient rooms lined one long hallway. When Laura was there, it was like a college dorm party. Forget the unsavory, discolored hospital food. They ordered out for lasagna, pizza, or salads from Cleveland's nearby Little Italy. They shared music, books, and card games—as much fun as they could sneak past the nurses station—but death was a frequent uninvited party-crasher. During Laura's lifetime, the average lifespan for a person with cystic fibrosis had dramatically increased to mid-twenties. She was in her mid-thirties when we met; she was a veteran survivor and had helped many face their final days.

The second summer after Bruce died, we went out for dinner one night while she was out of the hospital. We also toured the new house she was having built and ended up back at her old house, chatting on the bed in her bedroom, just like schoolgirls.

The computer was on a desk opposite the bed.

"What are you afraid of?" she scolded me. "You've already lost everything."

"Go ahead and shoot then," I said.

She focused the digital camera. "Do you want your boobs in the picture or not?"

"Not." I tried to smile instead of grimace. She shot my picture and immediately uploaded it to a Christian singles site.

And that was how I met Tom—because of Laura, my Naomi, of sorts.

She was right. I had already lost everything. I felt cut in half, my knees were badly scraped, my heart was broken, and I had nothing else to lose. The risks ahead of me were, with some common sense, mostly imaginary.

I entrusted my heart with my one tough girlfriend. Like Ruth's mother-in-law, Laura was godly and gritty rolled up in one.

We never know what cast of characters God will call into our lives; we only know they will be called and that our lives will be woven together in ways we would have never imagined.

*Go through the character qualities of Boaz highlighted in this chapter. Put a checkmark by the ones that are especially appealing to you.*

*Create a list of additional qualities you'd appreciate in a second husband.*

*What are some qualities your children would need or appreciate in a stepfather?*

*Do you have a Naomi or Laura in your life yet? Are you like a Naomi or Laura to any of your friends?*

*Maybe you won't get married again. Of course you've known that all along, but then again, maybe you will. There's no harm in being able to recognize your own Boaz when he enters the picture. And remember: Even if you fall down and scrape your knees or your heart, they'll eventually heal.*

Now to him who is able to do far more abundantly than all that we ask or think, according to the power at work within us, to him be glory in the church and in Christ Jesus throughout all generations, forever and ever. Amen. (Ephesians 3:20-21)

*Dear Lord,*

*You are able to do immeasurably more than all I can ask or imagine, and asking for a man like Boaz falls into that category! Please work according to your power that works within me. Transform me to accept the work you are doing in my life through the cast of characters like Naomi, Laura, and Boaz who may already be around me.*

*Amen.*

# Chapter Twenty

## *Glimpsing God*

Now Boaz had gone up to the gate and sat down there. And behold, the redeemer, of whom Boaz had spoken, came by. So Boaz said, "Turn aside, friend; sit down here." And he turned aside and sat down. And he took ten men of the elders of the city and said, "Sit down here." So they sat down. Then he said to the redeemer, "Naomi, who has come back from the country of Moab, is selling the parcel of land that belonged to our relative Elimelech. So I thought I would tell you of it and say, 'Buy it in the presence of those sitting here and in the presence of the elders of my people.' If you will redeem it, redeem it. But if you will not, tell me, that I may know, for there is no one besides you to redeem it, and I come after you." And he said, "I will redeem it." Then Boaz said, "The day you buy the field from the hand of Naomi, you also acquire Ruth the Moabite, the widow of the dead, in order to perpetuate the name of the dead in his inheritance." Then the redeemer said, "I cannot redeem it for myself, lest I impair my own inheritance. Take my right of redemption yourself, for I cannot redeem it."

Now this was the custom in former times in Israel concerning redeeming and exchanging: to confirm a transaction, the one drew off his sandal and gave it to the other, and this was the manner of attesting in Israel. So when the redeemer said to Boaz, "Buy it for yourself," he drew off his sandal. (Ruth 4:1-8)

*Dear Orpah,*
*    Naomi and I are wearing a rut in the floor pacing*
*back and forth while we wait to hear from Boaz.*
*    I could be married by sunset today!*
*                                    Wishing you were here,*
*                                                    Ruth*

# Glimpsing God

*Settling an estate? Ugh!* I'm glad my lawyer delighted in legalese and red tape; she made my life so much easier. We spent a couple afternoons passing papers back and forth. "This one is for blah, blah, blah…sign here," she'd say as she slid it across the desk. I'd scan it, try to look intelligent, scratch my name on the line, and slide it back. *Such mind-boggling drudgery! Does it really have to be so complicated?* Boaz, Ruth, and Naomi probably felt the same way.

Boaz dealt with estate settlement too. Scripture lays out his experience of gathering elders, waiting for the other kinsman-redeemer, and sealing the contract with a sandal. Although very different from today's ways, it wasn't very interesting then either. As I read this boring, strange, outdated page of Bible life, my mind objected, *So what? What's the big deal here? What does this have to do with widows today?*

But I found some good parallels for today in this peek at ordinary Bible life some 3,000 years ago. There were rules to follow and contracts to make. Although cumbersome, God orchestrated life pathways in the midst of these legalities. The pressure of the letter of the law was a refiner's fire, and from amidst those flames, the sterling character of Boaz surfaced. The traits he modeled are markers to keep us on the right path.

## Obedience to God

Boaz stayed within the law. He didn't have to, you know. Remember, this occurred during the time of the judges, when everyone did what was right in his own eyes! Boaz could have said, *"I'm buying Naomi's land and marrying Ruth and that's that."* Most people would have shrugged and said, *"Whatever,"* but Boaz wasn't trying to please society. He wanted to please God, so he obeyed God's stated rules for land redemption and widows.

## Patience

Secondly, Boaz had to sit down and wait for the next of kin to come along. He couldn't call, text, or send a letter. He just had to wait. Have you ever watched for someone special to come along in a crowd or for a car to pull into your driveway? I stand on tiptoes and crane my neck this way and that. Sometimes my heart starts to pound if I think I catch a glimpse of them.

Have you noticed there's a lot of waiting in the book of Ruth? Naomi had lived in Moab for at least ten years, the trip back to Bethlehem had taken four or five days, and Ruth had worked about two months before these events came together. Ruth and Naomi waited for Boaz, while Boaz waited at the city gate. There were plenty of opportunities for nail-biting, to be sure! In our day of instant messaging and fast food, we've lost the skill of waiting patiently, but these people remind us that it's a necessary part of life. They waited and they survived the waiting, and we will too.

## Openness

Once again there's divine coincidence in this story. God's works are often clothed in our ordinary routines. What do you think were the chances of the other kinsman-redeemer coming past Boaz that very day? Boaz could have been waiting for days but, behold!—*Surprise!*—the other kinsman came past. We take the arrival of this other relative for granted, but Boaz did not.

It takes a special sort of openness and mindset to see God's power in the many coincidences that play into our lives. Even in the drudgery of estate settlement, we rejoice over a number of providences. When we finally find a good lawyer, gather all the paperwork from the past—deeds, titles, liens, and wills—we need to notice God's fingerprints in those details and praise him for what has or hasn't been done. When we look back, we'll see that God's timing was perfect, even if our ability to see him was tested.

## Surrender

Boaz was willing to leave the outcome to God. He surrendered his own desire for Ruth and presented the case in a favorable way to the other relative as a great investment. The man immediately agreed to buy it.

Boaz must have gulped, for he'd just given away Ruth! But when he mentioned the other side of the deal, that it included Ruth and having children by her, the other relative resigned on the spot. It was common sense.

Let me briefly explain: It wasn't that this closer relative was afraid of marriage to Ruth for some unknown reason. The problem was with how his estate would have been divided between Ruth's children and his other children.[1]

If he had redeemed Naomi's land alone, as he had first assumed, his children would have all received equal portions of it. But with Ruth as part of the package, marriage to her would risk his current childrens' inheritance. They would have received nothing of Naomi's land; it would have all gone to Ruth's children. Additionally, his original family land would have had to be divided between his children and Ruth's children, leaving an even smaller inheritance for his children.

In summary, Ruth's children would receive all of Naomi's land as well as some of his. And his current family would receive a smaller inheritance. Everyone knew it would have been an unwise deal; no one would have expected him to jeopardize his current family. A sandal was exchanged instead of a deed, and the matter was honorably settled.

*Honor*

The mention of the sandal in this text may seem odd, but it demonstrated that Boaz was a man of honor and distinguishes it from another incident in the Old Testament.

In Deuteronomy 25:7-10, we learn of the shameful reputation of "The house of him who had his sandal pulled off." If a brother-in-law refused to marry his brother's widow, the widow was to bring him before the town elders and let them try to persuade him. If he continued to refuse, the widow publicly approached the man, took off one of his sandals and spat in his face! Boaz's initiative in redeeming Ruth circumvented this humiliation.

This vignette also shows us a much larger picture of law and grace. Old Testament law could have forced the other relative to be responsible for Ruth and Naomi. The law, intolerant and blind, demanded what he was incapable of performing without great jeopardy and burden. Old Testament law always proved man's inability to perform it, but through the generous and gracious work of Boaz, the weaker relative was spared. Likewise, we cannot meet God's standards on our own any better than this nearest relative did.

*Sacrifice*

Boaz paid a price to redeem Ruth and Naomi. His estate, like his relative's, would also diminish if he fathered children for Ruth, but he graciously accepted that burden in spite of the cost. He willingly agreed to pay the price. Choosing to obey God doesn't guarantee a free ride. It wasn't an easy thing for Jesus to redeem us either; the price of that was his death on the cross. Nevertheless, just like Boaz, he freely took us upon himself.

The generosity and willingness of Boaz to redeem the destitute Ruth and Naomi clearly resembles God's own love for us. We are helpless, we have no one else to turn to, and God himself saves and redeems us when no one else can or will.

Boaz's shoe swap no longer seemed like dull, strange or outdated drudgery to me. I related to Ruth and Naomi; we shared a common state. As they waited for news of redemption, I waited for comfort and rest. Around me swirled promises and possibilities. *Maybe this man or that man will come along and rescue me. Maybe once the estate is settled, I'll feel settled. Maybe this, maybe that...* And then I remembered how God clothes himself in the daily drudgery of duties that try my obedience, patience, openness, honor, surrender, and sacrifice.

I've learned to stand on my tiptoes, peeking out the window of my life. I watch for God, my Redeemer to break through the daily and mundane events crowding my life. I catch a glimpse, life quickens, and I think *. . . this day could change everything!*

*Are there days when you wish you could push a fast forward button on your life? Sometimes the hardest thing about daily life is that it's just so…daily.*

*If you need help getting started with the first steps of finding estate papers and budgeting, please visit my blog, <u>www.widowschristianplace.com</u> for some good links and resources.*

*What estate settlement tasks do you need to do?*

*Choose a date and time to start.* _____

*That's a great first step! Now, watch for God in the as-it-turned-out incidents that occur in the days ahead.*

*As you work through these details, which character traits do you think God will challenge you with most?*

- ❑ Obedience
- ❑ Patience
- ❑ Openness
- ❑ Surrender
- ❑ Honor
- ❑ Sacrifice

I t is good that one should wait quietly for the salvation of the Lord. (Lamentations 3:26)

*Dear Lord,*

*Are you really in the details of my life like you were with Boaz and Ruth? Open my eyes to the orchestrations and the coincidences that you are engineering on my behalf. My heart will stand on its tiptoes to watch!*

*Amen.*

# Section Five
# Blessing

# Chapter Twenty-One

## *Other Struggling Women*

Then Boaz said to the elders and all the people, "You are witnesses this day that I have bought from the hand of Naomi all that belonged to Elimelech and all that belonged to Chilion and to Mahlon. Also Ruth the Moabite, the widow of Mahlon, I have bought to be my wife, to perpetuate the name of the dead in his inheritance, that the name of the dead may not be cut off from among his brothers and from the gate of his native place. You are witnesses this day." Then all the people who were at the gate and the elders said, "We are witnesses. May the Lord make the woman, who is coming into your house, like Rachel and Leah, who together built up the house of Israel. May you act worthily in Ephrathah and be renowned in Bethlehem, and may your house be like the house of Perez, whom Tamar bore to Judah, because of the offspring that the Lord will give you by this young woman." (Ruth 4:9-12)

*Dear Mother and Father,*

*Today I received the greatest reward of my life! An important man here in Bethlehem married me today! His name is Boaz, and he's wonderful and kind. I'll be very happy and well off with him.*

*But here's the amazing part...The town elders pronounced a blessing over me! Me, a foreigner! Boaz told me all about it. I felt like they were giving me a royal crown. God has so much in store for Boaz and me...I've found a real home here.*

*Love always,*
*Ruth*

## Other Struggling Women

Boaz raised his kinsman's sandal to the sky and proclaimed his marriage to Ruth and the purchase of Naomi's property. As soon as the crowd of onlookers and town elders affirmed, "We are witnesses," the ceremony was over. Ruth was married without ever attending a wedding! She also received a powerful blessing that took hold and marked her in the pages of history.

The elders of Bethlehem lined Ruth up with three ancestral women: Rachel, Leah, and Tamar. "May the Lord make Ruth like them!" the elders proclaimed. What honor and prestige it must have bestowed upon Ruth the outsider, the Moabite! Rachel and Leah were founding mothers of the nation of Israel. Tamar was a mother of the tribe of Judah, Boaz's tribe. The blessing predicted that Ruth would be as influential, strong, and fertile as the founding mothers of the nation Israel and the tribe of Judah. We can liken it to a wedding toast for a bride marrying the next President of the United States or one who, her very self, might be the next President. It was very significant for Ruth, and it is very significant for us!

Furthermore, Boaz, as the bridegroom, was blessed with honor, influence, and respect from both his family and his village, in private and in public. Any who were not already aware of Boaz's fine reputation were now keenly aware of it. We can only liken him to a national hero.

The blessing tied respect for Ruth with honor and influence for Boaz, and then topped things off with good fortune and well-wishes that placed a special destiny and preeminence for their future children. "May your house be like the house of Perez," the townspeople and elders declared. (Ruth 4:12) Perez and the tribe of Judah rose to leadership in Israel, even though they were not the traditionally privileged firstborn in their families. Likewise, Ruth's children were blessed for a destiny of prominence and power in her new homeland.

In his book, *Shattered Dreams*, Dr. Larry Crabb asks deep questions about about this blessing. If Ruth was to become like Rachel, Leah, and Tamar, what was she really destined for?[1]

Life was hard and far from perfect for those women, so it is difficult to imagine why anyone would turn to them as symbols of blessing. Rachel and Leah were sisters, both married to Jacob, and they competed fiercely with each other to conceive children by him. (Genesis 29, 30)

Jacob passionately loved Rachel, but he was tricked into marrying Leah first. Rachel died during the birth of her second son and was buried near Bethlehem. Jacob mourned bitterly, but preceding his own death many years later, perhaps having grown to love his first wife, he asked to be buried with Leah. I hope you understand the epic romance and pain that went on between the lines of this brief summary.

Tamar came a little later. Like Ruth, she was a foreigner who married an Israelite and became a widow; however, Tamar had no Naomi. She was cheated out of welfare and family benefits by her brothers-in-law and her father-in-law; her life was threatened, and she was almost convicted of adultery and burned to death! She gave birth to twin boys and lived in a loveless marriage to her father-in-law, the twins' father, Judah. Scandalous, wasn't it? So why would the town elders choose Tamar, Rachel, and Leah as figures of blessing for Ruth?

The truth is, you don't have to have a perfect life to be a symbol of blessing. God uses struggling women to accomplish his purposes. In the midst of those struggles, when we are stripped of all crutches, façades, and power, we gain a valuable perspective on eternity, God, and our relation to life. Pain and suffering can make us more objective about life, sharpen our values, and—if we allow—develop a courage to live life with passion and drive as never before.

We share a bond with others who are suffering, a bond that puts us in the camp of those who "get it." My daughter Lisa once worked with a woman who'd lost both her husband and her children in a plane crash. When she found out that Lisa had lost her dad, she and Lisa shared an understanding. If the other women in their posh clothing store bemoaned that their skinny jeans didn't fit or their nail polish chipped, Lisa and Diane shared a knowing look, reiterating silently to one another something that they both know: *Life is far more precious than these trivial pursuits.*

This same wisdom spurred the act of the elders' blessing on Ruth, just like a knowing nod between Lisa and her co-worker and the silent fraternity of those who've suffered. In elevating Ruth to liken her to Rachel, Leah, and Tamar, I think the elders would say in today's words, "Ruth, you understand, you 'get it.' Your life hasn't been perfect, but you have put yourself in the place of God's blessing. We pronounce over you that in spite of the sorrow and suffering you've experienced, God will use you to lay a rich foundation for your family. He has a plan for your future. We'll never forget Rachel, Leah, and Tamar, and we'll never forget you."

It was a powerful blessing. Rooted in the reality of an imperfect world of sin, sickness, and death, it provided three treasures: true role models, the seedbed of community, and a future empowered by the Lord.

Aside from the occasional sneeze, we don't bless or get blessed enough these days. Why is that? Has money clouded our judgment so that we no longer see value in words alone? Is it that not enough of us "get it?" But let me ask this: If a godly person came up to you in private, asked permission to bless you, and then proceeded to gently place their hand on your shoulders and implore the Lord Almighty to bless you, would you value and remember that five years from now?

I've had two blessings as an individual, and I'll never forget them. The first was at a conference for pastors' wives, just two weeks after Bruce died. I was still in shock, mechanically doing everything on my calendar, so I attended even though I was no longer a pastor's wife, but a widow.

The dear director knew my story and asked if the group could pray for me. "Of course," I said. She had me come up to the podium with her, and she publicly prayed for me. After that, she dismissed the group for a coffee break, and that was when I was blessed.

I had noticed a stunningly beautiful African-American woman in the audience. She wore a sparkling gold caftan and matching turban. She looked like a magnificent queen. I, a skinny, dishwater-blonde, white woman, was awestruck. To the best of my recollection, I stood there paralyzed at the podium, unable to move for a moment. But then I noticed people weren't leaving the auditorium; well, actually, the white women were leaving, but the black sisters were all lining up. Oh my! It looked like a funeral receiving line, and I suppose in some way, that was exactly what it was.

On one hand, I dreaded it, but I also felt privileged that those African-American women, with a heritage of suffering almost woven into their DNA, were the ones to acknowledge me. The queen-lady in gold was first in line.

The flowing sleeves of her caftan enfolded me, and she drew me in. I felt like a stick and thought I might smother at first, but then I heard her low voice speak warm, rich words into my ear. They filled my head with eons of Israel's history and with God's presence and faithfulness; she was blessing me! She would say a Hebrew name of God and then bless me with it: "He is Elohim the Almighty. May you know his almighty power... He is Jehovah-jireh, the God who provides. May you rest in his provision... He is Jehovah–shalom, the God of peace. May his peace reign over you..."

I've thought of that blessing many times since. I've wondered who that woman was, how she came to know the names of God, and why they were so familiar to her. They were more than well-learned Sunday school lessons; they flowed from her heart.

In II Corinthians 1:4, we read, "We can comfort those in any trouble with the comfort we ourselves have received from God." I believe the queen-lady was doing exactly that: passing down the comfort and blessing she had once received.

Suffering is our initiation to true comfort. Countless women from the past and present welcome you into the exclusive fellowship of widowhood. The blessing of their struggle and perseverance, whether it's their story you've heard or their actual words whispered in your ear, is a priceless gift along the way.

*Would you allow me to bless you like the town elders blessed Ruth, like the queen-lady blessed me?*

Dear Woman Loved by God,

May the Lord God of Naomi and Ruth build you up in faith in his mighty power.

God is Adonai, "Master" or "Lord." His yoke is easy, and his burden is light. May you find his rest for your soul.

God is Elohim. He is "Strength" or "Power." The sovereign God, the strongest power of the universe, extends his faithful promises to you. May he be your strong tower and shelter from the storms of life.

El-Shaddai! God is "Almighty," the source of all blessings. May you experience the goodness and faithfulness that flow from his hands. His grace is sufficient for you.

Jehovah-rophe, "Jehovah heals." God himself will one day wipe away your tears and heal your brokenness.

Jehovah-jireh means "the God who provides." His eye is on the sparrow, and he clothes the lilies of the field. You are worth far more to him than these! He will provide for you. May you praise him for meeting your needs at just the right moment.

Jehovah-shalom, "the God of peace" be with you. He loves you and will provide a peace that passes understanding.

May the Lord God show kindness to you, my sister. May you find a place of rest and kindness in a field of favor.

Amen and amen.

# Chapter Twenty-Two

*Our Illusion of Control*

So Boaz took Ruth, and she became his wife. And he went in to her, and the Lord gave her conception, and she bore a son. (Ruth 4:13)

*Dear Mother and Father,*

*By the time this note arrives you will be grandparents! Yes, I am great with child. I had given up on ever being a mother, but it looks like my dream will come true, my empty arms finally satisfied.*

*I'm feeling wonderful and the midwives agree that an uncomplicated delivery and healthy baby are on their way. It's a boy, they say, from the way I carry.*

*How I long to see you and to watch you hold and enjoy your grandson, but the God of Israel, Naomi's God, has been good to me. I hope someday a young man will knock on your door. When you open it, he will say, "Grandma? Grandpa? I'm Ruth's boy. I'm here to meet you."*

*Love always,*
*Ruth*

# Our Illusion of Control

My brother Joel told me a robin was singing at the cemetery while Bruce's casket was drawn out of the hearse and we picked our way across crusty patches of snow and circled around it for our last goodbyes. I didn't have the energy to throw a rock at that bird. I didn't even hear it. But I sure wanted to smash it! *How dare it sing as if my husband is not gone, as if my world has not crumbled!* Yet I was so helpless that I couldn't have even hit it if I'd have wanted to. If you've seen me throw a baseball, you know I wouldn't have come close. I could never have reached that bird; I could never have found a way to control or shush it.

When I take a bird's-eye view of my life now, I see there's still not much I can control. Let's say I'm in a science class, and the assignment is to graph my life along a nice, straight baseline of "normal." My lifeline would see a series of ups and downs, hills and valleys. It would start out nice and straight—"normal"—until I turned sixteen. At that point my parents moved, uprooting me and throwing me into a high school culture that was something like a paper shredder. I held on tight as the line on my graph plunged downward. Two years later, the line shot upward when I happily escaped to college. Then it plummeted again when my grandma died; went up when I married Bruce; up at ministry opportunities; and peaked even higher with the birth of each one of my children. Between all those mountaintops, though, there were valleys of conflict, money troubles, more funerals, and struggles with trusting God . . . up, down, up, down, up down, like a spastic hospital heart monitor. Sound familiar? Why? Because control is an illusion, my friends!

I've never heard a sermon about Ruth's life being out of control, about all her helpless ups and downs, but I know she experienced them. She probably married Mahlon, Naomi's son, when she was around fifteen years old. She experienced infertility with him, and by the time she was twenty-five, she'd already been thrown into the role of a childless widow. Then she left her homeland and moved to Bethlehem with her angry and bitter (but full of faith) mother-in-law. She knew deep poverty, hard work, and extreme risk. She also knew rescue, redemption, and romance. And then, God enabled her to conceive. A graph of Ruth's life

*205*

wasn't level, peaceful, or anything close to "normal." It zigged and zagged with peaks and valleys, one right after another. We get so caught up with her romance and redemption that we often lose sight of the real Ruth, a woman full of heartaches, struggles, and questions. We also lose sight of the Lord, the one who conceived not only *her* story, but also the little life sprouting within her.

I think if I ever meet Ruth in heaven and ask her about those days, ask her if she ever wished she would have had more control, she'll be stunned at such a question. What a concept: that *we* control the events of our lives! For some reason, we think that we decide *if* we'll get married, *if* we'll have children, and *when* we'll have those children. We imagine *we* can choose what college we'll go to, what career field we'll find satisfaction in, and what the storybooks of our lives will say. What would happen if I were to sit down with Ruth and blurt this out: "Didn't you hate widowhood? Didn't you wish you'd had more control over your life?"

I'm sure her silence would be so heavy that I'd get a little uncomfortable. And then —then, I think she'd start laughing. Not mocking or demeaning me, but a silvery delight of a laugh. Like a woman caught in the silliness of a scene, the absurdity of life, she will hold her sides and giggle and laugh until tears stream down her face.

Then she'll wipe away those tears of laughter, catch her breath, take my hand and say, "Well, bless your heart. Bless your little heart! Aren't you adorable?" (Ruth must have been from *Southern* Moab). She'd try to catch her breath and go on, "I haven't thought like that for years."

I would want to point out, "Of course you haven't. You've been all restful and happy in heaven for thousands of years." I, on the other hand, fresh from my miserable existence on earth, would still have some questions on my mind. "Why don't things work out like they're supposed to? Why did you—and I—have to go through all the ups and downs? Why didn't God just let you marry Boaz in the first place? Why didn't you get to have any children with Mahlon?" My questions would tumble out, tripping over each other.

A sober and understanding look will shadow across her eyes. She'll sit up a little straighter, smooth a hand across her knee, and smile at me kindly. She'll glance behind me and then lift her chin to greet a man coming to join us: Mahlon.

Mahlon will kiss Ruth lightly and sit down next to her. "Everything worked out perfectly," he'll tell me.

Boaz will join us, then Obed, Naomi, Kilion, and Elimelech. Across the way I'll see Bruce coming toward us, along with Marilyn, Tom's first wife. Then will come my grandma and my girlfriend Laura, each holding my unnamed, miscarried babies and grandbabies in their arms.

"The Lord enabled her to conceive," Mahlon will remind me. "All the times Ruth and I tried to conceive, all the tears, all the disappointments, the hard times, the famines, all the lack of control we worried about had purposes greater than our own—just like that bird singing in a cemetery. There was something bigger, something outside. Something good was going on!"

As I think of this scene, my imagination fails, and like a dream, it all vanishes. Mahlon's words lead me back to my keyboard and the Bible open before me. Ruth and everyone else blink back to just names imbedded in a paper history now. Yet, there is something to the question of control, where it comes from, how it clouds our sight like a fog and fails to hold anything of substance.

The words of the psalmist tell me that just as God enabled Ruth to conceive, so, too, was I conceived. If I can believe anything from Psalm 139, I understand that God created my inmost being. *He* knit me together in my mother's womb. All my days—days of jagged peaks and valleys and the yearned-for flat, normal, peaceful days—have been ordained for me. Somewhere, God wrote them down before one of them ever occurred. One of those pages in God's story of my life tells the tale of the day when I will give up my illusion of control. I still might want to throw a rock at the robin singing in the cemetery, but on that day, it will be a little easier to let it sing.

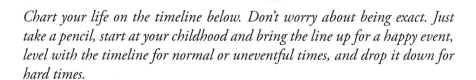

*Chart your life on the timeline below. Don't worry about being exact. Just take a pencil, start at your childhood and bring the line up for a happy event, level with the timeline for normal or uneventful times, and drop it down for hard times.*

0_____ 25_____ 50_____ 75 _____ 100 years

*Do you have some peaks and valleys?*

It's humbling to see this bird's-eye view of life. We realize exactly how little control we have over what our lifeline looks like. We have very little say over the events that pattern our days or the monotony that flatlines them.

Sometimes the only way to get any sense of the whole thing is to see life as just that: a little series of hiccups and spasms on a scrap of paper. Now, take that scrap of paper (either actually cut it out of this book, copy it onto another paper, or imagine this in your mind) and put it in your hand and wrap your fingers over it.

Your hand is larger. Your hand is stronger. Just like God's hand is so much larger and stronger than any of ours. When we put our life in Christ's hand, he holds us, and the Father holds him. When we're in God's hands, our lives—every peak and every valley—are under control: God's control!

In that day you will know that I am in my Father, and you in me, and I in you. (John 14:20)

*Dear Lord,*

*Help me realize that when I asked you to come into my heart, you accepted me into yours. Nothing is out of control. Something much larger is going on, in you. Thank you for holding me; I am in you, and you are in me.*

*Amen.*

# Chapter Twenty-Three

## *Opening Our Arms*

Then the women said to Naomi, "Blessed be the Lord, who has not left you this day without a redeemer, and may his name be renowned in Israel! He shall be to you a restorer of life and a nourisher of your old age, for your daughter-in-law who loves you, who is more to you than seven sons, has given birth to him." Then Naomi took the child and laid him on her lap and became his nurse. And the women of the neighborhood gave him a name, saying, "A son has been born to Naomi." They named him Obed. He was the father of Jesse, the father of David. (Ruth 4:14-17)

Dear Orpah,

I woke up before daylight this morning. Well, how could I sleep with noisy girlfriends calling and knocking at my door? And there — I could hardly believe it — there there was my grandson! Ruth sent him right over here! God bless her!

He's so beautiful! Perfect and whole and healthy! No signs of famine in this baby! It's lovely to hold him. He smells so good! He's so snuggly and peaceful.

Orpah, I'm madly in love! I've come alive! I feel love again!

As I cradled him in my arms he looked right into my eyes. Imagine that for a newborn — but he really did! It was like he was saying, "I'll take care of you, Grandma."

We all agree he must be famous in our land. And my girlfriends even named him! I'm not so sure I approve, I love the name "Jesse," but they named him "Obed," which means "servant of God." It's a good name, strong and faithful. You must come see him!

Love,
Naomi

# Opening Our Arms

Naomi held a newborn baby in her arms, and she learned something as he looked into her eyes: *Good things can still happen.* Her girlfriends assured her that her little grandson would renew her life and care for her as she aged. Naomi accepted the baby, drew him to herself, and became his primary caretaker.

God has the uncanny ability to distill goodness out of the worst disasters when we are willing to open our arms and hearts to receive them as Naomi did. He's comfortable with paradigms: with grandmothers serving as mothers, with widows finding new love, with faith as an action rather than a feeling. He's the Man of Sorrows, yet he is always rejoicing.

How can God contain and engineer what we consider such irreconcilable differences—joy and sorrow, life and death, faith and despair? Is it because he takes each life and makes it a story, because he's the author and he knows the ending?

We get caught up in wanting our story to be that of the princess and Prince Charming, living happily-ever-after with our perfect children in a perfect dragon-proof palace. We would all choose a cookie-cutter life that looks just like everyone else's: safe, predictable, indulgent…

But God, the literary artist, bursts into our life and turns it into an amazing story full of miracles. Miracles aren't always what we wish: that we are healthy, strong, beautiful, rich, and happy-ever-after. God's miracles are of a much higher order. "Eye has not seen, nor ear heard!" (I Corinthians 2:9)

Sometimes he writes chapters into our lives in which the biggest miracle is that we still trust him. That, like Naomi, we pick up our broken hearts and shattered dreams and determine to put one foot in front of the other until we find God and his place of blessing and redemption. The true miracle is that we go to him when we're certain he has abandoned and attacked us or knocked us off our swing. It's a miracle in and of itself that we turn to him, and return to him, just as we are, full of complaints and bitterness. It's a miracle that we wait and watch for our redemption, no matter how long it takes.

Naomi knew that each struggling step was a miracle. First, she knew it in her head. Her head, not her heart, told her feet to take her back to God. Faith is not "following your heart." Faith is following God because he is God. Had she listened to her bitter, angry heart, she would have died weeping over the graves in Moab. Once her feet got her back to the place of redemption, her heart began to heal.

Remember how Naomi changed at the sight of the barley Ruth brought home to her the first day of harvesting? That was the day Naomi's faith moved from her head to her heart. When she opened up to see God's provision, her deep root of bitterness began to melt away. Before that, she'd been cultivating the bitterness mentioned in Hebrews 12:15: "See to it that no one fails to obtain the grace of God; that no 'root of bitterness' springs up and causes trouble, and by it many become defiled."

When Naomi quit giving in to the thought that she deserved to be bitter and instead spoke the blessing and gratitude we read about in Ruth 2, she traded the bitter root for a whole different kind of root.

In the final chapter of God's story, Revelation 22:16, we catch a glimpse of the full miracle Naomi received when she opened her arms. Jesus stated, "I am the root and the descendant of David." When Naomi gave up the bitter root in her heart and replaced it with gratitude, the grace of God watered the root of King David in her family! God ordained that she would raise her grandson Obed, who would father Jesse, who would father David, who would become the king of Israel, in the lineage of the King of Kings, Christ Himself!

As Naomi gazed upon the grandson in her arms, she had no idea that a seed of such royalty rested on her knee. In her lifetime, she never learned that the Messiah would come through her influence. Not having a grandfather to share the joy of little Obed's first tooth, first step, or first word was painful. Not having grandchildren through her own sons, Mahlon and Kilion, might have tempted her to be jealous of Ruth's happiness or resentful and overly sensitive about perceived slights.

Although she could trust that God would take care of her and could hope for the best, just like us, she made daily choices and struggled with temptation. Perhaps she had the haunting sense of waiting for the next horrible shoe to drop. *What if baby Obed dies?* The world still wasn't safe, and Naomi knew all too well that there was always the chance of pain and heartache paying an unexpected visit, even in the best of times.

Still, Naomi made the daily choice of accepting the grace of God in the form of baby Obed. When she opened her arms and embraced the infant, she embraced God's grace, and God gave her a purpose for living that has spanned the centuries, reaching us even today. That's what I call a good thing—and yes, even a miracle.

We're not so very different from Naomi or Ruth. When they arrived in Bethlehem, the barley harvest was ready to begin. We have a harvest to work as well. Jesus said, "Look, I tell you, lift up your eyes, and see that the fields are white for harvest." (John 4:35) The fields are still out there, and the harvest still needs widows who will, step by step, move their feet to find God. Widows who will open their heart to praise him, and accept whichever form of his grace appears in each day. Widows who will open their arms to a baby, another widow, a new husband, or a hen-pecking, Paparazzi-like crowd of neighbors who won't let her wallow in grief or change her name to "Mara."

When we get stuck in grief over the past, we devalue the present. We easily overlook and miss the touches of new purpose God sends our way. There are co-workers, friends, and family at hand, and God has put them around us for a royal reason. Could it be that, like Naomi, we are left to raise royalty, the people of his glorious kingdom?

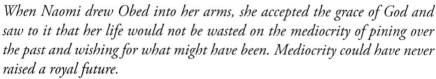

*When Naomi drew Obed into her arms, she accepted the grace of God and saw to it that her life would not be wasted on the mediocrity of pining over the past and wishing for what might have been. Mediocrity could have never raised a royal future.*

*What sort of future do you envision for yourself and the people God has entrusted you with? Have you embraced the people God has sent your way? How will you bless those people and enable them to righteously rule the world?*

*Name the people you are surrounded by:*

*Which of them are God's gift of grace to you?*

*What is one thing can you do today that will help raise up generations of God's royal kingdom people as your legacy?*

*Do the same thing tomorrow and the next day and the next....*

*If you honestly have no one in your life right now, there is a world full of opportunity waiting right outside your door! Please swing that door open and have a look around! Start at your church. Ask your pastor about short-term mission trips or local organizations. Visit Widows Christian Place (www. widowschristianplace.com) and get involved with GriefShare and the other organizations and support groups I've listed there.*

B ut you are a chosen race, a royal priesthood, a holy nation, a people for his own possession, that you may proclaim the excellencies of him who called you out of darkness into his marvelous light. (I Peter 2:9)

*Dear Lord,*

*I lift my arms to receive your grace. Open my eyes to gaze upon my future. Help me fulfill the purpose and legacy that you have left me here to accomplish. Good things still happen, Lord, and I thank you that I am part of your plan.*

*Amen.*

# Chapter Twenty-Four

*Belonging*

"This then, is the family line…" (Ruth 4:18 NIV)

*Dear Orpah,*

*Bethlehem and my story are part of a distant past now. I remember everything perfectly, but back then, it looked as if my earthly life had been pinched into a small, broken picture frame covered with a thick dust of loneliness and grief.*

*Now I see my life in the large, magnificent framework of God's design for eternity. My sadness has slid into the shadows of my portrait. Like artistic brush strokes, loneliness and grief accent the rich undertones of my silver-streaked hair and shade the contours of my crimson robe. The dark days of my life have added depth and dimension to the wilderness landscape behind me. I must say, "It's a masterpiece!" Leonardo, a nice man I met here in Heaven, told me it surpasses his "Mona Lisa." He sees the artistry, too.*

*How could I have ever known that stepping out of Moab would be such an important link in God's plan of salvation not only for me, but also for the entire world?*

*The fissures of loneliness and bitterness that nearly shattered me when I broke down at the entrance to Bethlehem, crying "God is against me!" have been filled and healed over by love and new life. My family tree is full and, oh how it has grown and keeps on growing!*

*Love always,*

*Naomi*

# Belonging

The book of Ruth closes with a genealogy, something like the scrolling of credits at the end of a movie. Before the house lights come on and we walk out of our theater, let's consider why such a lovely story would end with a family tree.

These closing verses of Ruth are the book's final clue for a widow seeking true happiness and joy, hope, and purpose. A widow's cure for loneliness and the prescription for joy is found in family and legacy: the epitaph on our tombstone and our notch on the family tree record our people and place—the spot of love on the earth where we belonged.

Do you despair at the thought of empty, lonely years ahead of you? Does your house overwhelm you with memories and silence, holding no promise for joy to once again fill its halls? Please don't give up! You're in chapter one of your grief, just as Naomi was when she cried out in bitterness, loneliness, and misery.[1] But, if you put one foot in front of the other and determine to live in God's promises, the pages will begin to turn. You'll move on to the next chapter, and someday your arms will hold the fulfillment of joy and God's purpose for you. He longs to bring you into his full satisfaction and delight. He does so through the framework of family: "God sets the lonely in families." (Psalm 68:6 NIV)

Let's look at three aspects of family groups. If you battle loneliness like many widows do, let's uncover your own particular fit and options.

*Natural Family*

These, of course, are the people related to you by blood or marriage vow: parents, children, siblings, cousins, aunts, uncles, and in-laws.

If you have children at home, you cannot expect them to fulfill your needs for companionship and adult conversation, but I like what my wise friend Myra said on my blog, Widows Christian Place: "In saving your kids, you save yourself."[2] If you're a mom, fulfilling the role God has given you will bring you great reward.

If you are caring for aging parents or relatives, God will certainly see that you reap what you sow and connect you to those who will care for your future needs. Also, remember that God uses our needs to drive us to increase our faith and seek his provision for those needs. Remember the three choices for widows exemplified by Orpah, Naomi, and Ruth: remain, return, or risk. Perhaps you should move closer to family members or open your home to them. I know of widows with children at home; these women have asked their own mothers to move in with them, and everyone—mom, daughter, and grandchildren—have benefitted from such arrangements. This doesn't work for all personalities, of course, but maybe it's something you can consider.

What are the pros and cons of getting closer to your own family? What should you realistically consider and pray about before suggesting this to your family? Pastor and author Max Lucado has said, "Don't make a decision in a storm that you wouldn't make in calm weather."[3] When riding the stormy seas of grief, do not take in an alcoholic, abusive, or lazy relative. Instead, prayerfully consider your reasonable options.

*Extended Family*

Perhaps you should create an extended family under your own roof. If you have the means, financially support children around the world through missions like Compassion International, care for foster children, or consider adoption. During my daughter Lisa's senior year of high school, one of her girlfriends lived with us for several months. I found that the added laughter and antics were a delight and joy to me. Muriel, a widow in my church, asked her grandchildren to spend summers with her during their college years.

If you need help with your mortgage or rent, consider subletting or finding a boarder. Widowed authors Elisabeth Elliott and Jerry Sittser each mention boarders they've had at various times.[4, 5] Or why not share house and housing expenses with another widow? A certain friend and I have talked several times in the past of how we will be the Christian version of the old TV show *Golden Girls* if we ever find ourselves widowed at the same time. Just draw up contracts, boundaries, and expectations that you can agree to ahead of time and expect periods of adjustment. With the right people involved, having a boarder or sharing a house with other widows could be a great arrangement.

*God's Family*

"God sets the lonely in families," and he also sets widows in the greater context of his community of believers. Did you know that God ordered widows as a priority for the nation of Israel in the Old Testament and again for the church in the New Testament? When God introduced these covenant relationships, he always made sure that widows were included early on and given priority.

For Israel, Exodus 22 listed a series of crimes and consequences. "If a man does this, then he must pay that," was generally how it went, listing offense after offense, along with its resulting punishment or payment. If the crime was committed against a widow or orphan, the perpetrator was in real trouble! Exodus 22:22-24 warns that those who take advantage of widows and orphans will arouse the anger of God himself! He doesn't leave vengeance for the widow up to mere law and the government of man to accomplish! Oh, how he watches and cares for each with a jealous and guarding eye!

God watched over widows in the New Testament too. The first group of church leaders appointed after the twelve apostles were seven men "full of the Spirit and wisdom." (Acts 6:3) And what was the mission of these seven? They were responsible for the distribution of food *to the widows.* Among them was Stephen, the first Christian martyr. The finest of the church's finest were chosen to serve the widow! In God's eyes, nothing is too good for the widow when he is in charge of the organization. Reality falls far short in our world and in churches today, but I point this out to show you the intent and heart of God toward widows and what to aim for.

This often overlooked passion and care of God for widows culminates in an obscure verse that I believe has been the secret of surviving and thriving for many widows who know Christ. Isaiah 54:4-5 says, "Fear not, for you will not be ashamed; be not confounded, for you will not be disgraced; for you will forget the shame of your youth, and the reproach of your widowhood you will remember no more. *For your Maker is your husband,* the Lord of hosts is his name; and the Holy One of Israel is your Redeemer, the God of the whole earth he is called."

As I think back on Naomi in chapter one of Ruth, it's possible that fear held her in Moab for the ten years after her husband died. She also felt shame, disgrace, and humiliation in a culture where a woman without a husband or children was considered invisible and nameless. Yet by chapter four, Naomi had a baby grandson and a daughter-in-law who loved her and was "better than seven sons." (Ruth 4:15) Her arms were full; her name, "my joy" had been restored. She knew the Holy One of Israel as her Redeemer, and perhaps she even knew her Maker as her husband, as mentioned in Isaiah 54:5.

It's quite a phrase: "Your Maker is your husband." It's a difficult concept to accept for many widows. A friend who reviewed this book before it was released told me, "A Heavenly Husband is hard for most widows to understand. It took me several years." I must admit I shied away and refused such a thought when I was widowed. Remember my reaction when I found out there were thousands of new widows around the world every day and I thought God only had one verse for them? I didn't appreciate the idea at all! Plus, growing up in a predominantly Catholic area, the kids around me had always mentioned that nuns were "married" to God, and the idea seemed too strange. But I've learned much since then, and this verse in Isaiah is a far healthier and holier concept than memories from my childhood and my own reasoning.

Maybe this will shed some light on "a heavenly husband:" it certainly helped me. My oldest daughter, Brooke, got married a year and a half after her dad died. Bruce had known and loved the man she was marrying, so I felt he would approve, but it was very hard to go through such a milestone without my husband beside me. I'm pretty independent and secure when I'm by myself, but when I'm in a crowd of people, I'm always looking for a face I recognize, a hand to hold, a familiar group to slip into.

Much to my extended family's horror (but okay with my children), I invited a male friend of mine to the wedding. Peter, a total extrovert who is at home with anybody or in any crowd, was perfect for the assignment. When I was busy with receiving lines, family pictures, and last-minute touches, I didn't worry that he'd be off moping and feeling sorry for himself in some corner; he was busy talking to anyone who'd listen! But when

I found myself alone in the middle of the banquet room, when my heart started racing and panic starting to rise in my throat, I could scan the crowd and home in on Peter. He was there; he always had his eye on me, watching out for me and ready to come to my aid, almost like a steady, comfortable, reliable husband of many years.

That is what "Your Maker is your husband," foundationally means. Just as Pete was watching out for me, God has his eye on the widow. He's always there, watching and ready to aid. From the induction of the nation of Israel to the organization of his church, God has made it plain that he passionately cares for the widow. He's a widow's defender, shelter, and fortress. God protects and provides. He gently leads her, and he lovingly stands watch. Woe to those who come against her, for her Maker IS her husband!

"God sets the lonely in families," and he declares his special passion for the widow. Any individual can know they are important to God, but a woman who is cast down to the bare-boned identity of "widow" carries a unique opportunity to understand her important status and relationship in God's eyes. Like Naomi, she grows from her first chapter of grief's emptiness and despair to her chapter four of fulfillment found in family, extended family, and God's family. She belongs! She has a home, and she's found kindness and rest; her refuge is secure in the heart of her Protector and Maker, God Almighty.

*Our journey with Naomi and Ruth, two women who lost everything, has seen us "through many dangers, toils, and fears" like the hymn "Amazing Grace" states. We've seen the dangerous wilderness and dark grief they experienced, and we've also seen their extraordinary hope. I hope you look forward to meeting them in eternity as much as I do. Truly, their example shows that God intends life after death not only in a heavenly sense for the husband who died, but also for the widow he left behind!*

*As you think back to when you first opened the cover of this book, how have you yourself changed since chapter one?*

*Fill in the letter on the following page. You may address it the same way you did in chapter one.*

# Chapter Twenty-Four

Dear _____,

I'm pretty extraordinary, like Naomi.

Here's what my life is like now:

I live in_____.

My family members are_____
_____

I might invite these needy children, other widows, or boarders to be part of my extended family:
_____
_____

In God's family, although others may not realize it, I am in a position of honor, esteem, protection, and love.

People describe me as
_____

The best way to describe my race is that I (circle one)

Run          Walk          Limp          Stagger Crawl

I have no idea what the future will bring, but here's how I feel about it:
_____
_____

From_____

Date:_____

Fear not, for you will not be ashamed; be not confounded, for you will not be disgraced; for you will forget the shame of your youth, and the reproach of your widowhood you will remember no more. For your Maker is your husband, the Lord of hosts is his name; and the Holy One of Israel is your Redeemer, the God of the whole earth he is called. (Isaiah 54:4-5)

*Dear Lord,*

*I praise you and thank you for your love, protection and care for me. I'm amazed and filled with wonder that you'd call yourself my husband. Continue to teach me all about this relationship with you and your good plans for me. Continue to heal my brokenness and grief as I trust in you and follow your good plans for me.*

*Amen.*

# Chapter Twenty-Five

### *Heaven's Shore*

If they had been thinking of that land from which they had gone out, they would have had opportunity to return. But as it is, they desire a better country, that is, a heavenly one. Therefore God is not ashamed to be called their God, for he has prepared for them a city. (Hebrews 11:15-16)

*Dear Orpah,*

*I never did make it back to Moab to visit you. To be honest, although I longed to see you, I longed for this fair country even more. I could not bear to leave God's promised land. I could only look forward, never back.*

*I still do, even now. It's thousands of years later and I continue to look ahead. I've seen the Messiah in my lineage, prophecies fulfilled, and God's rich redemption. I've seen how my own life foreshadowed it all, promising welcome to God's family for every outsider and foreigner willing to believe. Yet, here in Heaven there's always more to come. Blessings and grace unfold every day!*

*I've come into far more than I ever dreamed of finding in Bethlehem. God's promises and provisions are revealed in new and marvelous wonders day after day, moment by moment. This glorious eternity swells with God's loving presence and this astounding place.*

*Truly, his faithfulness endures forever and his mercies are new every morning!*

*Love,*
*Ruth*

## Heaven's Shore

We're all driven to this final chapter. We naturally seek rest, resolution, and the happy ending of a last page. When Naomi prayed for kindness and rest for Ruth and Orpah, she was praying for such satisfaction. God had given her exactly what she'd asked for, and he provides the same to widows today. It's a two-part comfort—a person and a place. As I mentioned in the last chapter, God promises the person of himself in a husband relationship with the widow. It's all about belonging: God belongs to the widow, and the widow belongs to God.

Secondly, God provides a place. God satisfies our yearning for comfort and belonging with not only his person, but with his place—our eternal, heavenly home. All the classic happily-ever-after stories are instinctual to us for this very reason. It's as if God has hard-wired us with an internal desire to know and experience the complete satisfaction, peace, and glory of belonging to him and being with him in the home he's preparing for us.

Many ideas and dreams of heaven fall far short of the real place. Did television cartoons you watched as a child impress fluffy white clouds and golden harp caricatures of heaven on your mind? Or now, as an adult, is your view of God's place limited to sentimental goose bumps about chumming around with loved ones at a great big family reunion? How about singing in a heavenly chorus to infinity and beyond?

No matter how grand our imaginations of that very real place, they fall so short of what heaven truly is. Our God is limitless! His creativity is infinite! Floating on clouds and strumming harps might be nice, but really, wouldn't that get a little boring after a while? Sure, I will love spending time with my passed-on loved ones. I'd love to sing with a choir, but for all of eternity? God has much more in store!

Every once in a while, I catch a glimpse.

After Tom and I got married, we spent several summer vacations on Lake George in Ticonderoga, New York, where Tom's parents still live. Lake George is almost 30 miles long, a couple miles across at points, and dotted with over 300 islands. Mountains with granite outcroppings dip their feet into it. Crystal clear, spring-fed waters fill this deep wonderland. Miles of it are environmentally protected, and even where there are homes and cabins, the landscape is densely lined with tall pines, blue spruce, bright maples, and white birch. In short, it's magnificent!

We rented the same cabin every year and invited extra family and friends. Fun was the order of things around the clock. Sleeping bags lined the living room floor at night, and the grill was fired up daily. Water toys, beach towels, and plastic floats littered the lawn to the dock, where the boat or jet ski were at our disposal.

Sometimes Tom and I even had a few days all to ourselves. On one of those rare private days, we motored the boat out to an island for a picnic, then anchored out a way and spent a quiet afternoon swimming, sunbathing, and reading. Near dinnertime, we leisurely pulled anchor and headed the three or four miles back to our cabin.

As we cut around one of the mountains and turned to the north end of the lake, dark purple clouds and a stiff breeze surprised us. We could only hope to race home before the storm. Tom ran our ski boat across the waves as fast as he could, but then it hit: A wall of rain came at us, chopping the water with large yellow-white drops, slapping our faces and stinging our eyes as we churned through. Just as we turned the boat into our bay, the rain diminished; when you're racing north as fast as you can and the storm is pushing south, it doesn't last long. A light shower petered out to a mere sprinkle as we pulled the boat alongside the pier.

Wringing out towels and t-shirts, we tossed flip-flops and coolers out of the boat. There were still a couple hours before sunset, so we knew things had a chance to dry out before sundown. Patches of blue sky were already breaking the clouds; the leftover sprinkles wouldn't hurt anything.

As I stepped out of the boat, Tom was already halfway up the hill with our stuff. I planted both feet firmly on the pier and brushed my wet hair off my face, when suddenly, everything changed. I remember looking across our boat, across the bay, and up at Cook Mountain. It all looked so different—clear and rain-washed, almost sparkling—yet so much bigger. Up the entire tree-covered side of the mountain, the tips of the pine needles glistened with drops of rain dancing down from one branch to another.

It was as if all the oxygen molecules had suddenly expanded and started to shimmer. The air grew iridescent. Objects took on a twinkling dimension: The posts of the pier, blades of grass along the shoreline, and two birds flitting across the water all stood out in a surreal moment, projected beyond a third dimension. Then it hit me: *I'm standing in a rainbow!* More quickly than a breath, everything around me had changed character. Earthiness became ethereal, air became color, and in that twinkling of an eye, I realized heaven could be that close.

*At my last heartbeat, that is all it will take. Just one last breath, and I will be there. My foot will step on heaven's shore as surely as my foot had stepped out of that wet boat and onto the pier. Earth's veil will lift like a shadow's passing moment.*

*We will not spend eternity endlessly lazing around on clouds, strumming harps, or chumming around with long-lost loved ones, lovely as that might seem. With Naomi, Ruth, and the saints of Hebrews, I will welcome my new home from a distance. I look forward to the new heaven and new earth described in Revelation. I will know even as I am known. I will explore, adventure, and learn to new depths of understanding. I'll joyfully glorify and praise Almighty God, my Creator and Redeemer.*

With all those thoughts rushing through me, my heart beat faster as the shining prism of color moved across the pier and out onto the water again.

Tom called to me, and I hurried up the hill. There, above Heart Bay, we watched the rainbow arc from one end of the sapphire bay to the other, traveling with the clouds, beaming the shores, its presence oblivious to the people seeking shelter from the storm.

Life is not safe. The unthinkable happens in this world saturated with sinfulness. We cry and will continue to be hurt; we seek shelter from the rain and fail to see the rainbow. We're lonely, but we are not alone. God exists! He is with us. He has a plan and purpose to accomplish by raising up widows for the generations to come. Extraordinary hope can ignite when we realize our new place in this earth and in the new earth to come, where God will wipe away every tear. Now we know in part, but then we will know all that we need to know.

On that day, we'll be home, right where we belong, safe and secure at last. With our kindness received, our rest complete, we'll be fully satisfied.

This is the hope and the purpose I have learned from Naomi and Ruth: to let God love me with his faithful grace and amazing mercies and to prepare for the day when his glorious presence and place will be completely mine. Come quickly, Lord Jesus!

*Look at what Jesus prayed in John 17:24 (NIV) and fill your name in the blank:*

"Father, I want _____to be with me where I am, and to see my glory…"

*Can you begin to imagine that incredible day?*

*God has given us a few clues and pictures to fire our imaginations about heaven. The best thing I can do for you is to mention some of them here, ask the Holy Spirit to illumine you, and encourage you to learn more about your future home.*

*Read Revelation 21 for a peek at a bit of heaven, the New Jerusalem.*

In Revelation 21:16, note the shape of the city. _____. This is much larger in size, but the shape is exactly the same as the Holy of Holies in God's plan for the tabernacle, reflecting God's presence and holiness in the New Jerusalem.

The city is 1,200 stadia in length. Check the notes in your Bible, ask your pastor, or search online to find out how many miles that will be: _____ miles.

Write down the length, width, and height of the city in miles:

Length _____ x Width_____ x Height_____

*Here in the United States, you can grasp a bit of the enormity of this city by drawing a square. Use New Orleans, Louisiana as your first point. Draw the line north and well into the province of Ontario, Canada. Then go west to the city of Vancouver, Canada, south to the Baja Peninsula in Mexico, and then back to New Orleans. Consider today's wonders in this area: the Rocky Mountains, Yellowstone, The Grand Canyon, Lake Superior, and the Mississippi River, just to mention a few; think about the cities, regions, and people.*

*Keep in mind that there is a whole planet, the new earth, beyond this city! (Revelation 21:24)*

From Revelation 21:19-20, list the gemstones that decorate the wall.

Compare the length of the wall to the largest wall we know of today, the Great Wall of China.

There's so much more! How thick is the wall? _____feet. (Revelation 21:14 NIV)

How big a pearl would be needed for a gate in a wall that size? What is the city itself made of? _____

*This incredible city will be the eternal dwelling of God's family. Why not start looking forward to it now? What is the first thing you'd like to do when you arrive in your new home? Who are the people you will look for? Which of the beautiful things in the New Jerusalem will you want to explore first? May God bless your anticipation and fill you with his life-giving hope as you set your heart on these things above.*

May the God of hope fill you with all joy and peace as you trust in him, so that you may overflow with hope by the power of the Holy Spirit. (Romans 15:13 NIV)


*Almighty God,*

*You know my affliction, weakness and loss, yet you want me. You're preparing an amazing, beautiful place for me, a glittering city beyond my wildest dreams because of your immense and glorious love. I'll finally be home, where all longings and heartaches will find peace. Thank you for your abundant kindness, rest, and hope for my grieving heart.*

*Amen.*

# Acknowledgements

A few years ago I began reading acknowledgement pages that other authors had written, and I was always surprised at the number of people who had influenced and helped them in the labor process of bringing their thoughts and ideas to life as a book. I was a little envious that they had so many good friends and such input into their product. I was afraid that my own acknowledgment page would be meager and lean. Yet now, when I actually wonder who to acknowledge, I find I know exactly where to start, but I don't know where to stop! Please bear with me as I indulge my deep gratitude for the generous care, influence, and love I've been blessed with during the time of my bereavement and now as I pass along the comfort I've received.

This book and anything I could possibly do for widows all stem from my deepest gratitude to my own Redeemer and God, the Lord Jesus Christ. Without God and his Word, I'd have no story to tell. I thank Riverview Church and friends in Novelty, Ohio for their love, watchcare, and generous support when we were all reeling with grief. I dare not begin to name anyone—that'd be another book!

My family—Mom, thank you for saying, "Oh, my baby," before you choked up when I called and told you Bruce died. Dad, you were my strong tower; Steve, Joel, and Anjee, aunts, uncles, cousins—you came hundreds and hundreds of miles with your wonderful mates and stuffed-full-of-kids minivans—which was just what I needed. My Bowman family, the love lives on! I'm so thankful you never let go of me and the kids. Brooke and Chris, Lisa, Brad, Aaron—you always seemed to admire me and support me in my writing ventures and that meant so much to me. My Hardy family—your love and acceptance welcomed me like family right from the start, helping me understand how secure Ruth must have felt.

My husband, Tom, who patiently supported and believed in my doing this for six long years, put up with several weeks apart, invested plenty of money, held me when I cried, and never once grumbled or complained—you are my rescuer and gift from God. What an incredible blessing to have had "one true love" twice in my life.

In the writing of this book, many thanks to the ladies of Riverview Church who enthusiastically participated in my Bible study on Ruth. That was the seed for the book. God watered it at Montrose Writers Conference, in Montrose, Pennsylvania, where I pitched it to writers and editors and received such good direction and advice. Special thanks to Grace Fabian, Jennifer Sands, Sarah

Hampshire, Cynthia Bezek, Carol Wedeven, Elaine Miller, Bob Hostetler, and Virelle Kidder.

Further thanks to Dr. Charlie Dyer, for fielding my questions over the years with his biblical expertise; to Todd Bolen for generously sharing his photograph and developing the website www.BiblePlaces.com. Thanks to the other writers who've helped me along the way: Lois Pecce and Dayton Christian Scribes; also Cindy Heflin, Cindy Steffen, and Marlena Graves. And to my manuscript readers: Kelly Creason, Shearon Lehrack, Candy Feathers, Miriam Neff, Amy James, Barb Parkhurst-Oakes, Connie Frederick, Carol Montgomery. To my many Internet friends who inspire me with their lives and offer me the deep privilege of walking the widows' path alongside them, my heart is yours.

# Notes

## Introduction—How This Book Came About

1. Joseph P. Shapiro, "Enjoying Life After Death—Once sidelined, widows are making the golden years better for everyone," U.S. News & World Report, Vol. 129 Issue 10 (September 11, 2000): 76.

## Chapter 1—When the Unthinkable Happens

1. I searched and searched to find a reason why Elimelech and Naomi ventured to Moab. If they were farmers, it seemed doubtful to me they'd purchase farmland in Moab and raise crops. If they were shepherds, it seemed likewise doubtful that a single family's flocks would survive such a journey during drought and famine. But an ancient village supported various trades, and I began to wonder if, like the virtuous woman of Proverbs 31, perhaps Naomi made fine linen. Or maybe Elimelech was a potter. When I discovered that The King's Highway, a thriving ancient trade route, went right through Moab, I conjectured that taking their crafts to the most prosperous city in Moab, Kir-hareseth (modern Kerak), and trading their wares along the King's Highway would be a reasonable option for them. But this is only my own theory. I've yet to find any other speculation. For further background on Moab and The King's Highway: Todd Bolen, "Moab and Edom." *BiblePlaces. com, http://www.bibleplaces.com/moabedom.htm* (July 30, 2012)

2. Robert L. Hubbard, Jr., *The New International Commentary on the Old Testament: The Book of Ruth*, (Grand Rapids, Mich.: Wm. B. Eerdmans Publishing, 1988), 89.

## Chapter 2—Leaning into the Wind

1. No one knows what Mahlon and Killion died from. Some sources say their names meant "sickness" or "weak," so they died of poor health; but other sources say the names have no meaning, or are unknown. Since the survival rate for a sick baby in ancient times was very slim I think it's unlikely their names meant they were sickly. I also can't imagine any mother naming her newborn "Sickness" or "Weakling!" But, this far removed from the day, we don't what the boys names meant, and we don't know how they died. Perhaps they were sick, but

then again, perhaps they died at the hand of man. The image of Naomi rocking her sons' blood-soaked robes is my way to raise awareness and respect for the mothers of military and civilian young men who die at the hand of man; my heart goes out to these women every day.

2. Hubbard, *The Book of Ruth*, 96.

## Chapter 4—Mountains of Loneliness

1. I had quite a discussion about Naomi and Ruth's journey with some of my readers. Some focus group participants assumed Naomi and Ruth had traveled in a caravan or that they followed the exodus route into Israel and crossed the Jordan River north of the Dead Sea. I found nothing published about the route Naomi and Ruth traveled back to Bethlehem, so I once again asked Dr. Dyer. He informed me that "the common mode of transportation at the time was walking, and walking required the shortest distance. If Naomi and Ruth started out from the ancient Moab city of Kir-hareseth there were two routes to take. They could go north along the Kings Highway and then turn off it and go west: cross the Jordan River, go to Jericho, then Jerusalem, and turn a bit south to Bethlehem, a distance of 77 miles. Or the other route went west to the narrowest point of the Dead Sea. They would wade across (or walk across on dry land if the water level was lower) and go north to Bethlehem via En Gedi and the wilderness of Tekoa, a total distance of approximately 55 miles." When I consider the shorter distance, plus the fact that God had to miraculously divide the water of the Jordan River when the nation of Israel had to cross it, the route along the Dead Sea seems most likely to me, too. In the Ryrie Study Bible is a comment in I Sam.22:3 that David took his parents ". . . to Moab, across the Dead Sea." There is also evidence that the Romans constructed a road through that part of the Dead Sea. Although Roman use was centuries later, it lends further credibility of its ancient use.

## Chapter 5—Two Needs of Every Widow

1. I Kings 11:7

2. Jennifer Sands, A Tempered Faith, (Savannah, Georgia: The Olive Press, 2003), 135.

3. Miriam Neff, "Church Resources/What Churches Should Know," *Widow Connection.com, http://www.widowconnection.com/Help/Help/cr.html* (July 30, 2012).

4. Hubbard, *The Book of Ruth*, 105.

5. Miriam Neff, "Church Resources/What Churches Should Know," *Widow Connection.com, http://www.widowconnection.com/Help/Help/cr.html* (July 30, 2012).

## Chapter 6—Choosing Light or Lies

1. Hubbard, *The Book of Ruth*, 113.

2. Rob Turner, from a sermon at Apex Community Church, Dayton, Ohio. (Summer 2007).

3. Melissa Fry, from a women's retreat at Riverview Church, Novelty, Ohio. (March, 2005).

## Chapter 7—Three Choices

1. Hubbard, *The Book of Ruth*, 120.

## Chapter 8—Faith Steps In

1. Hubbard, *The Book of Ruth*, 117.

2. Andree Seu, "A grieving primer—Postcard from a friend going through the shadow of death," *World*, Vol. 14 Number 20 (May 22, 1999): 33.

## Chapter 10—Brokenness

1. Hubbard, *The Book of Ruth*, 126-127.

2. Larry Crabb, *Shattered Dreams—God's Unexpected Pathway to Joy,* (Colorado Springs: Waterbrook Press, 2001), 64-68.

3. Cornelius Hancock, from a sermon at Springboro Baptist Church, Springboro, Ohio. (Nov. 8, 2009).

4. You will not find a verse in the Bible that states Mary was a widow, but

it has been accepted for years in church tradition. Presumed by the absence of any mention of Joseph after Jesus was twelve-years-old, (Luke 2:41-52), and by the necessity of charging John with her care, (John 19:27), it seems quite likely and offers an interesting speculation.

**Chapter 11—How Will You Survive?**

1. Miriam Neff, "Moving Forward/Facts About Our Finances," *Widow Connection.com,* *http://www.widowconnection.com/Moving%20Forward/Moving%20Forward/Moving%20Forward/faof.html* (July 30, 2012).

2. Elisabeth Elliot, "Do The Next Thing," *Back to the Bible, http://www.backtothebible.org/index.php/Gateway-to-Joy/Do-the-Next-Thing.html* (July 30, 2012).

**Chapter 12—A New Identity**

1. Hubbard, *The Book of Ruth*, 138.

2. Hubbard, *The Book of Ruth*, 148-150.

3. Although Boaz may not have given Ruth exactly what she asked for, Ruth 2:11-16 tells of his further and very gracious benevolence to her. I urge you to look into the lovely interaction between Boaz and Ruth on your own.

**Chapter 13—Mysterious Kindness**

1. Hubbard, *The Book of Ruth*, 179.

2. Ibid.

**Chapter 15—Taking Refuge**

1. Judith Nichols Moore, speaking at Widows International Rally & Leaders Training at Park West Church of God, Knoxville, Tenn. (Nov. 6, 2010).

2. Ibid.

3. Miriam Neff, *From One Widow to Another—Conversations on the New*

*You,* (Chicago: Moody Publishers, 2009), 33-46.

**Chapter 16—Facing the Future**

1. Hubbard, *The Book of Ruth*, 199.

**Chapter 17—Protecting Virtue**

1. Hubbard, *The Book of Ruth*, 203.

**Chapter 18—Trusting God in the Dark**

1. Hubbard, *The Book of Ruth*, 213.

**Chapter 19—Recognizing Your Boaz**

1. Hubbard, *The Book of Ruth*, 213.

2. Hubbard, *The Book of Ruth*, 222.

**Chapter 20—Glimpsing God**

1. Hubbard, *The Book of Ruth*, 245.

**Chapter 21—Other Struggling Women**

1. Crabb, *Shattered Dreams*, 136.

**Chapter 24—Belonging**

1. Ferree Hardy, "Myra's Story, part 2." *Widows Christian Place: http://www.widowschristianplace.com/2010/10/circle-of-friends-myras-story-part-2.html* (July 31, 2012).

2. Ferree Hardy, "Do's & Don'ts for Widowhood & Other Unthinkable Circumstances." *Widows Christian Place: http://www.widowschristianplace.com/2011/06/dos-donts-for-widowhood-other.html* (July 31, 2012).

3. Max Lucado, *Max On Life: Answers and Insights to Your Most Important Questions,* (Nashville: Thomas Nelson, 2010), 187.

4. Elisabeth Elliot, "About Elisabeth," *Elisabeth Elliot: http://www.elisa-bethelliot.org/about.html* (July 31, 2012).

5. Jerry Sittser, *A Grace Disguised—How the Soul Grows Through Loss, expanded edition*, (Grand Rapids, Mich.: Zondervan, 2004), 79.

# Contact Information

I hope you feel like you've made some new friends because you've read this book—Naomi, Ruth, and me! Let's stay connected at my blog, Widows Christian Place, where you'll find help and encouragement for the rest of your journey. Plus you'll find an excellent, free book club discussion guide for *Postcards from the Widows' Path* posted there. No special training is necessary to form a book club. Just invite some friends over and use whichever questions you want to prompt a good discussion that will deepen your friendships and your walk with God.

Please visit me at www.widowschristianplace.com, email me at WCplace@gmail.com, or friend me on Facebook! I look forward to getting to know you. You've heard my story, and I'd love to hear yours.

To order more copies of Postcards from the Widows' Path, please visit the Greyden Press Bookstore on-line at http://www.greydenpress.com/store/.

## Artwork Used in Layout of Book

Cover: Tissot, James. *Ruth Gleaning.* 1896. Oil on canvas.

Page 63: Doré, Gustav. *Ruth and Naomi.* 19th century. Engraving.

Page 79: Blake, William. *Ruth and Naomi.* 1795. Oil on canvas.

Page 135: Tissot, James. *Ruth Gleaning.* 1896. Oil on canvas.

Page 211: Solomon, Simeon. *Ruth, Naomi and the Child Obed.* 1860. Wood engraving on India paper, from *Dalziels' Bible Gallery.*